Priest's Hut—S. Cuthbert's.

Frontispiece.

Sketches of Kafir Life

(With Illustrations)

By Godfrey Callaway

Mission Priest of S. Cuthbert's

With Preface by

The Right Rev. Alan G. S. Gibson, D.D.

Coadjutor-Bishop of Capetown

NEGRO UNIVERSITIES PRESS

NEW YORK

Originally published in 1905
by A. R. Mowbray & Co., Limited, London

Reprinted 1969 by
Negro Universities Press
A DIVISION OF GREENWOOD PUBLISHING CORP.
NEW YORK

SBN 8371-1277-X

PREFATORY NOTE

THIS little book has been written during an enforced rest in Switzerland, and it owes much to the kind help of friends who will not, I know, wish to be mentioned by name.

Any proceeds will be given to the Building Fund of the new church at S. Cuthbert's.

My best thanks are due to Miss E. M. Wigan for the photographs which have supplied the illustrations.

G. C.

PREFACE

A BOOK such as this surely needs no Preface; it speaks for itself. May one not say that it is like one of our up-country South-African houses, as we see them on so many of the farms in the Western Province of Cape Colony? You open the door, and you step straight in, with outstretched hand, sure of a hospitable welcome; it is no porch, or hall, or vestibule into which you have entered, but you are right in the house itself; and, as you look around, everything tells you that you are in the heart of South-African life.

And yet, when a dear friend, whom fourteen years of common interests and hopes have bound very closely to one, asks for a Preface, how is it possible to refuse? It is true that the addition may mar the artistic symmetry of the building; but, after all, there is this consolation. Is it not the case that part of the charm and the interest of a house lies just in those very irregularities and additions, each of which has its own tale of character, and tastes, and age? At the very least, if this Preface serves no other purpose, it will show how complete is the sympathy between past and present workers at S. Cuthbert's; that in spite of the changes and developments that time must bring, there has been no breach of continuity, and no consciousness of differences.

It has always seemed to me a matter of the greatest difficulty to convey to those who have never been in South Africa anything like an adequate picture of the life out there. Letters or speeches may give very accurate descriptions, as far as they go; but much remains in the background of the writer's or speaker's mind, not touched upon just because to him it is so familiar, but unknown to the stranger to whom he is trying to depict the whole life as it really is; and the absence of this makes the picture not only imperfect, but, it may be, actually misleading.

It is largely because I see in this book a real representation of so much of the true life of that country where my own home has been for more than three-and-twenty years, that I rejoice so greatly at its compilation. I cannot but feel that the writer, called away by ill health from the work which is so dear to him, and for which he is so admirably fitted, is finding by his pen another way in which to win for the souls he loves the sympathy and the prayers of many, and to call others into that harvest-field where the labourers are so few. I do not know of any other book that has so truly caught the spirit of Kafir life. As you read, you are conscious that the atmosphere of the veld is all about you, and the wonderful spell that South-African life exercises is upon you. What it is no man can perhaps exactly say. Even the lover of the veld, who loves it for its own sake, as he tries to put its message into words, seems to be struggling to utter the unutterable; but, whatever it is, there it is, a force to be reckoned with, something with its own distinct influence, a part of the life. There, then, is the atmosphere of the book; and within that the reader passes rapidly from scene to scene. He sees the clashing of the old system and the new, and he begins to understand something of the bewilderment that this, like all transition periods, must necessarily bring with it. He

catches a glimpse of some of the problems that beset the
work of the missionary: polygamy, with the countless
practical difficulties that it brings in its train ; witchcraft,
an ever-present factor in Kaffrarian life, however it may
be explained ; linguistic troubles, such as every new-
comer is bound to face. He sees something of the
trader, whose position is, judged from the highest stand-
point, one of the hardest on the face of the whole earth ;
and he rejoices to think that the trader is so often a help,
and not a hindrance, to the work of the Christian
missionary. The further he reads, the greater is his
confidence in the writer ; for he learns that failures and
disappointments are not concealed, and that the story of
Mtshazi stands side by side with the story of Augustine.
So, as page after page is turned, the reader is at last
enabled to understand some of the features of the Kafir
character ; and to see how much there is that is lovable,
and how much (in spite of very many differences) that is
like the white man's life. The writer does not, of course,
profess to be exhaustive. He might have told us stories
to illustrate the love of parents, the boundless hospitality,
the loyalty to the chief, the devotion to the white master,
the sensitiveness of conscience, which are all true marks
of the Bântu race. Or he might have turned to the
other side, and have let us see (for some lines that he
has written in *Marita* show that he knows it well :
indeed, how could one who has worked as a missionary
for fourteen years, and been in charge of so large a work
as S. Cuthbert's, fail to know it ?) something of the awful
blackness that lies on heathendom. But what he has
told us is perhaps enough ; enough, at any rate, to whet
our appetites, and make us ask for more.

To me the book has a special, personal interest; for many of those of whom the stories are told are my own much-valued friends. Kanyelwa, the self-taught preacher, whose excellent work dates back to the days of Bishop Key; J. M., and J. M., and Marita, whose development it has been such a happiness to trace in these pages; Chelston, who, in all his wanderings, never altogether lost touch with his old missionary, but would still write to me from time to time; Isaac Magudu, the most fervent evangelist of his race that I have ever known; Mdunyelwa, whose son Lohana ran away from S. Cuthbert's because he thought he was bewitched; Nomlala and his family; above all Mtshazi, who had all his father's attractiveness and his father's weakness, drawn away (as I cannot but think) from the right path in some measure by his mother's influence, herself a renegade—the chief who, one hopes, may still be brought back to God by discipline and many prayers: these were all so well known to me that I cannot but rejoice to think that they should be allowed, through the medium of this book, to speak to others.

The writer has mentioned more than once the 'South-African Native Affairs Commission' (1903–5). Many laymen have often spoken and written in the most cordial terms of missionary work. During my twelve years in the Transkei (1882–94) I do not recall a single magistrate who did not, from his own personal experience of the results of missions, give his support to missionaries. The testimony of the late Mrs. Bishop is very familiar to the English public; and there are, perhaps, few persons who have written with more sympathy, common-sense, and knowledge than Sir H. H. Johnston in his *British Central Africa* (chapter vii, 'Mis-

sionaries'). But the witness of our own Commission is
probably unique. It was composed of twelve laymen,
all experts, the chairman being Sir Godfrey Lagden.
Six states were represented, the Cape Colony, Natal,
Orange River Colony, Transvaal, Rhodesia, Basutoland.
The sittings extended over a period of some two years,
and evidence was taken from every side. The findings
of the Commission were not always unanimous; but on
the subject of missionary work there was entire unanimity.
This Preface cannot, perhaps, have a better conclusion
than the quotation of part of what the Commission says
(p. 55) on ' Christianity and Morals ' :—

'For the moral improvement of the natives there is
available no influence equal to that of religious belief.
The vague superstitions of the heathen are entirely
unconnected with any moral ideas, though upon sen-
suality, dishonesty, and other vices there have always
been certain tribal restraints, which, while not based
upon abstract morality, have been real, and, so far as
they go, effective. These removed, civilization, particularly in the larger towns, brings the native under the
influence of a social system of which he too often sees
and assimilates the worst side only. . . . The Commission
. . . is of opinion that hope for the elevation of the native
races must depend mainly on their acceptance of Christian faith and morals. . . . It is true that the conduct of
many converts to Christianity is not all that could be
desired, and that the native Christian does not appear to
escape at once and entirely from certain besetting sins of
his nature : but, nevertheless, the weight of evidence is in
favour of the improved morality of the Christian section
of the population, and to the effect that there appears

to be in the native mind no inherent incapacity to appreciate the truths of Christian teaching, and to adopt Christian morals as a standard.

' *Resolution :—*

'(*a*) The Commission is satisfied that one great element for the civilization of the natives is to be found in Christianity.

'(*b*) The Commission is of opinion that regular moral and religious instruction should be given in all native schools.'

ALAN G. S. GIBSON,
Bishop-Coadjutor of Capetown.

LONDON, *September* 21, 1905.

INTRODUCTION

THE following sketches can hardly appear without a few words about S. Cuthbert's Mission, in which I have gained all my experience of Kafirs [1] and Kafirland. A brief account of the Mission and of the journey by which it is reached appeared recently in the *Cowley Evangelist*, and this will now serve well as my introduction.

We disembark at East London—a port lying between Capetown and Durban, and, after forty miles by train, we begin a journey of 180 miles by post-cart. This is accomplished in two days, with about eighteen changes of mules. After sixty miles of this drive we cross the famous Kei River, which was, until comparatively recently, the northern boundary of the Cape Colony, and we now enter the Diocese of S. John's, Kaffraria. This was only formed as a separate diocese in 1873, when Dr. Henry Callaway was consecrated as the first bishop.

The whole extent of the diocese is about 35,000 square miles, and it contains a population of 826,000. The Europeans number only a small percentage of this total, and, except in certain farming districts specially reserved for them, they consist mostly of Government officials, missionaries, and traders. The natives are of various tribes, but, with the exception of some Basutos

[1] I use the word Kafir in its loose sense, as applying to all the tribes of the Bântu race (including Fingo) in the Transkei.

(who are not numerous in S. John's Diocese), they all speak the Xosa language, and the tribal distinctions in this territory are not very great.

After crossing the Kei the whole country is full of interest. Along the road we pass numbers of waggons with their teams of sixteen to eighteen oxen, driven mostly by Kafirs, and loaded with produce (grain or wool) going down to East London, or returning with provisions for the traders.

In all directions, dotted about on the veld, or perched up in the kopjes, are the 'kraals' of the natives, and at many of these we see either the heathen in their red blankets or the dressed (not necessarily Christian) people sitting about.

Here and there you catch signs of buildings which are more or less obviously churches, or schools, or traders' residences.

We reach Umtata at one p.m. of the second day, and as we look round upon all the iron roofs of a European township, we try to remind ourselves that Umtata has already acquired quite a venerable place in the ecclesiastical history of the Transkei.

In 1877 Bishop Callaway decided to make this place the site of his cathedral, and before long, by his remarkable energy, he had established there a strong centre of spiritual and educational work. A new pro-cathedral has recently been built in the place of the old iron building which was in use all the days of Bishop Callaway and nearly all the days of his successor, Bransby Lewis Key.

We also see the solid beginnings of a cathedral proper, rising up on a good site in the European part of

BOYS (BOARDERS) BEATING OUT MEALIES.

To face page xiii.

the township, and close to this is the Diocesan Girls' School (English).

Close to the pro-cathedral is S. John's College—a large institution, where over 100 native boys are boarded and educated, and on the other side is S. Bede's Theological College, from which we hope, in course of time, to draw a never-failing supply of native catechists, deacons and priests.

But we are not allowed to spend long in Umtata, and at two p.m. we are summoned by the bugle to take our seats in the post-cart. Twenty-seven miles more, and we reach the little European village of Tsolo. This village receives its ministrations from S. Cuthbert's, and we notice a nice little stone church, newly built by native workmen trained at the Mission.

From Tsolo we have a drive (not by post-cart) of nine miles, and we pass through a large part of the country occupied by the tribe of Pondomisi, amongst whom S. Cuthbert's Mission is situated.

Just before the light fades away we reach the last shoulder of the Bele Mountain, from which we look down upon S. Cuthbert's. Here let us pull up, while I briefly point out to you the various objects of interest.

This is the mother-station of a parish, which now corresponds in area with the magisterial district of Tsolo. Only ten years ago it was nearly five times its present size *in area*; but, as the work increased, it has been gradually reduced. Even now, in addition to the large educational work at the mother-station, there are twenty-two different centres of work in the outlying district, and a few small centres for English services.

But all this outside work is as yet invisible to you,

and what you see in front of you is the mother-station only—called by the natives 'Ncolosi', and by us S. Cuthbert's.

One border of the Mission land runs along the very spot upon which we are halting. The whole extent of this land is about 4,000 acres. Originally it was the gift of the chief of the Pondomisi, but subsequently the Government confirmed the gift and it became diocesan property, held in trust for missionary purposes.

Scattered about over the whole extent of this land we see the kraals of the Christian people who are settled upon it, with their ploughing lands below them, sloping down to the streams.

Right in the centre of this Mission land is a plot of about 200 acres, which is recognized as the glebe, and upon the higher part of which you can see the Mission buildings, &c. Let us begin at the lower end and look at these in order. First, there is the little cemetery with its lych gate, and modest Calvary. Above this is the 'Cottage', where our lady-workers live, with various other buildings of a humbler character clustering round it, which are chiefly used to accommodate girl boarders. Above this again, and separated from it by a little plantation of trees, is the old parsonage—now chiefly used for guests.

To the left are many huts, where our boy boarders live, watched over, to some extent, by our laymen, who live in similar huts close by. Up again, above the old parsonage, are the school buildings, where some 180 children assemble daily, and the carpenters' shop, from which much work is turned out, and more is always wanted. Beyond these is the little church, of very mean

GIRL-BOARDERS' HUTS.

To face page xiv.

exterior, but with reverent—though primitive—interior. Here on Festivals and some Sundays we are most inconveniently crowded.

Beyond the church are the walls of the new church, which is so much needed and so long in coming, and, behind these, are the Community buildings, which have only been occupied for three years. . . .

Twenty-five years ago, if we had stood at the same spot, we should have seen only bare veld where now the Mission buildings are standing. We hope that what we now see is the outward sign of a change which has taken place in the hearts and lives of numbers of the people.

GODFREY CALLAWAY.

LIST OF CONTENTS

LIST OF ILLUSTRATIONS

SKETCHES OF KAFIR LIFE

CHAPTER I

THE VELD

WE are taught that all Nature bears a message to us from the Unseen—that it half reveals and half conceals God Himself.

> ' For I have learned
> To look on Nature, not as in the hour
> Of thoughtless youth. . . .
> And I have felt
> A presence that disturbs me with the joy
> Of elevated thoughts: a sense sublime
> Of something far more deeply interfused,
> Whose dwelling is the light of setting suns,
> And the round ocean and the living air
> And the blue sky, and in the mind of man
> A motion and a spirit, that impels
> All thinking things, all objects of all thought,
> And rolls through all things.'
>> Wordsworth's *Lines above Tintern Abbey.*

But Nature has many moods, and a many-sided character. Just as every nation is to make some special contribution to the whole character of redeemed humanity, so each aspect of Nature has something distinctive in its message, some special note which goes to make up the harmony of the whole. In each aspect is 'a motion and a spirit that impels all thinking things.'

We may conceive of Nature in every country as trying to whisper its special message into the ears of man. She will not rest until he hears it, for it is he who must utter that message in new and higher ways. So Nature goes on whispering until at last man listens, and catches, and expresses. She whispers to the architect, to the artist, to the musician, to the poet, to the mystic, until each in turn tries to express that special note, and add it to the harmony of the whole.

The veld too must have its special message, but it is strangely elusive. A friend of mine who is a great lover of things beautiful, feels that for him it has no message. Its vastness oppresses him, and he sighs always for a little bit of England. We sat one day upon a lofty mountain, looking down into wide, undulating stretches of veld melting away into dim and distant hills. Presently my friend turned his chair round, away from the great expanse, to look instead at a bit of the solemn forest close by.

> 'Your ghost will walk, you lover of trees
> (If our loves remain)
> In an English lane,
> By a cornfield-side a-flutter with poppies.'
>   Browning's *De Gustibus*.

Surely it cannot be that the veld has no special note! The message must be there, and it awaits the lover's inspiration, whether he be poet, or musician, or mystic.

> 'But GOD has a few of us whom He whispers in the ear;
> The rest may reason and welcome: 'tis we musicians know.'
>   Browning's *Abt Vogler*.

But the musicians only know because they love, and the veld still awaits the insight, the inspiration of its true lover.

But are there no true lovers of the veld?

We think of the great ships coming from all the countries of the world to the shores of South Africa. We think of the crowded decks, of the feverish haste with which the daily sum of miles is counted. The great heart of the ship beats too slowly for these impatient travellers. At last the famous Table Mountain appears in sight, crowning the beautiful bay. But no time is to be lost in exploring its beauties. The luggage is collected, the tickets are taken, and off they are carried once more. Up they rush through miles and miles of the vast Karoo, until at last the veld is reached. But there they do not stop. It is not the veld they want, it is the gold that the veld conceals. Not among such as these may its true lovers be found.

We think, again, of the transport-driver, who spends many months of the year on the road with his waggon and sixteen oxen.

It is one of those brilliant star-light nights when the dome of heaven looks so immense. The quiet, patient oxen are lying down after the long 'trek', and the three-legged cooking-pot is planted over the little road-side fire. Hardly a sound is heard except the breathing of the oxen and the occasional crackling of the flames. Far away on the distant hills are the brilliant lights of a veld fire as it creeps up towards the top with serpentine movement.

Away on the ridges above the valleys are the countless little fires over which the women of the kraals are cooking the evening meal.

Who would not be a lover of the veld in such an hour? It must surely touch the fancy and stir the affection even of the transport-driver.

The Kafir, too, is a lover of the veld. There is a legend [1] current amongst certain tribes that the black man was first created, but that the Creator was not satisfied with His work. He reserved the best things for the white man yet to be created, and to the black man He gave only cattle, and assegais, and mealies, and Kafir corn.

When the pot of frothy beer is brought to him, the Kafir loves the veld and praises the rich soil which gives him his food and his drink. As he pours out the thick amasi (sour milk) from his gourd, he loves it for the succulent juices of the grass.

Again, he loves the veld as he watches his cattle and sheep coming in to his kraal at night, and he hears his friends say that none are so fat as his.

And other seeming lovers of the veld there are, who love neither its gold, nor its pasture, nor its soil. Yet their eyes glisten with tears as they think of it, and often they turn to the photograph on the table before them. It is only a tiny enclosure they see, with a few mounds, and miles and miles of veld all around.

But some one who was very dear to them found a resting-place there, and for them the veld is sacred ground.

But still the veld waits for its real lover. The lover must love it, not for its gold, not for the restful ease of a quiet night, not for its soil, not for its sacred burden of dust, but for itself. Until the lover arrives, the veld will not give up its message.

What does it say, this land of ' far-off distances ', of

---

[1] See Kidd's *Essential Kafir*.

clear air, of wondrous blue, of quick change, of violent storms?

Some of us have arrived at the threshold of love's sanctuary, but we have not yet entered in. Sometimes the curtain seems to be partly lifted, and we catch a glimpse which makes us long for a fuller revelation. We seem to see a face which speaks of the great issues of life. There is nothing little about it—all is on a large scale. It smiles radiantly, or it frowns vehemently; it hints of lavish treasure, or of stern and cruel want.

There is the suggestion of greatness, stretching away past the limits of man's vision into eternity. In the merely physical sphere man stands oppressed by this sense of greatness. It is borne in upon him that 'Man is like a thing of nought: his time passeth away like a shadow.' He shrinks away, and turns to his little patch of ploughed land and to his kraal on the ridge. He wraps his blanket more closely round him, as though for a moment a cloud had hidden the warm rays of the sun. He goes off to count his sheep on the mountain-side, and quickly all unwelcome thoughts are banished in the rich sensations of the present. But when man is conscious of the spiritual sphere and of his own relationship to it, then that sense of Nature's greatness suggests another answer to the question 'What is man?' He is impressed by the lesson of man's dignity—'Thou madest him lower than the angels: to crown him with glory and worship. Thou makest him to have dominion of the works of Thy hands; and Thou hast put all things in subjection under his feet.'

All low aims and mean desires stand rebuked. We are bidden to take a large view of life, and to face it from the stand-point of eternity. The 'far-off' is brought near. God's greatness and majesty are seen to be impressed upon the vastness of the veld.

But the 'far-off' contains both Heaven and Hell, and nowhere is this contrast so vividly symbolized as in the land of the veld. The changes there are surprisingly rapid, and the transformation strangely complete.

In the early morning no cloud is to be seen, and the sun touches all the mountain-tops with its glorious light. In the afternoon the blue sky has vanished, and heavy, black, thunder-charged clouds hang over us.

Is it to be wondered at that, in the spiritual sphere, the struggle is so intense, that the falls are so great, that the heights sometimes look so unattainable? We are insensibly led to expect great contrasts—terrible defeats and signal victories. Calvary and the Resurrection are seen to be very near, man's sin and God's forgiveness are in close relationship.

In the early morning the Presence of the Altar is with us, and Heaven is not far off. In the afternoon we are only conscious on all sides of the 'snare of the hunter', and the 'noisome pestilence'. We see the contrasts, we wait to see the harmony.

'On the earth the broken arcs ; in the Heaven a perfect round.'
Browning's *Abt Vogler*.

OCCASIONAL CUSTOMERS—SMALL BOYS CRICKET XI.

To face page 7.

CHAPTER II

THE TRADER'S STORE

WHAT can a trader's store have to do with missionary work? So I, too, might have asked before I went out to South Africa. My previous conceptions on this subject were very vague indeed.

When I thought at all of trade dealings between white and black, I pictured rather wholesale exchange in 'kind', when representatives of the Kafirs would come with cattle, skins, wool, and grain, to receive blankets, hoes, beads, &c. I never imagined that over innumerable counters would daily and hourly pass copper and silver coins stamped with His Majesty's image in exchange for the varied products of European factories. Still less did I think that the same counters would be, more than anything else, the medium by which Kafir thought and life become penetrated with European ideas upon every conceivable subject.

Directly you cross the great Kei River you find that, after the Kafir kraal, the most universal, the most prominent, and most magnetic object is the trading store. It is true that here and there it is overshadowed by the Government Court House or by the Mission Church; but I seriously doubt if either of these can claim the same share of attention in Kafir thought.

It may be urged that the influence of the traders cannot be compared with that of magistrates or missionaries. But it must be remembered that the magistrates

are all united in one common effort to uphold the aims
of the Government, and the missionaries are also united
in upholding the aims of Christianity.

The traders may be united in a common aim to do
a good business, but otherwise, in matters political and
religious, they are wholly divided and sometimes indifferent. If, alongside of their trading, they were united
in some common policy, political or religious, it is
doubtful if either the magistrate or the missionary could
exercise so great an influence.

Before I attempt to describe the Kafir trading store,
let me say something about the traders. For the most
part they are English (or English-Colonial) and Scotch,
but directly they settle down in Kafirland their old name
disappears and a new one takes its place. Kafirs are
very quick in picking out some characteristic which may
suggest a name, but sometimes any trivial incident may
serve the same purpose. ' Ujojuboya '—one who sniffs
at the wool,—' Ugxiba '—the tall man—were amongst
the names given to our neighbours in trading stores ;
and, in asking Kafirs the way to them, it would be of
little use to speak of them by their English names.

Let me introduce you to a trader's home before I
introduce you to his store. I must warn you that there
is quite as much difference between the homes of the
South African as there is between those of English
traders. They range from one room with discomfort
and penury, to the well-built house with good stabling
and every comfort.

It is a real pleasure to be sure of a welcome from my
friend the trader at S. M——'s. I have distinct, but hardly
pleasant, recollections of a certain Kafir hut in the same

neighbourhood in which I used to 'put up' before the arrival of my friend P——.

Even the native Deacon, who once shared it with me, groaned aloud, and seemed somewhat disturbed owing to the attentions of certain small residents who thought that sleep was an unworthy use of midnight hours.

'Oh! Mfundisi, I am weak, I cannot work to-day,' was the early morning greeting of my companion.

It is not quite with the same feelings of apprehension that one rides up to that nice-looking brick house quite detached and separate from the store. In front is a charming little flower garden, carefully tended by Mrs. P——. On the stoep is a collection of ferns, which would arouse the envy of many an English gardener.

By the time you have noticed these things, out comes P—— from his store, with smiling face and hearty welcome. In a few minutes more you are sitting in an easy chair on the stoep, and Mrs. P—— is pouring out a refreshing cup of tea for you. As you look into the sitting-room, which opens out on to the stoep, you see the evidences of comfort and refinement. After riding for ten or twenty miles through a country filled with Kafir kraals, it is a strange surprise to open a door, and to see a good piano—with a pianola for the unlearned!

But I venture to say that if you were a missionary in South Africa, however well you might relish the contrast between your present quarters and a Kafir hut for your own sake, you would relish it far more for the sake of your horse. Day by day that patient, willing animal has carried you about, and for many hours has been your only companion. It is not strange that a real intimacy springs up between man and beast. Few things make one so ashamed of oneself as the fits of impatience when spurs or whip are too freely used, but I verily believe the horse generally understands when one asks for pardon.

With all the goodwill in the world, there are some occasions when it is impossible to do anything for the poor horse's comfort, and those are the occasions when the missionary suffers. Think of a cold, wet night at a Kafir kraal when you cannot find any place to shelter your horse, nor is a bundle of forage to be obtained for love or money. There is nothing for it but to knee-halter him and let him do the best he can for himself. In vain you try to sleep as you hear the poor beast rubbing up against the sides of the hut, trying to get a particle of shelter.

What a comfort beyond words it is to hear our friend P—— now give a royal order for mealies and forage! What a joy to go into the stable and to see the good horse standing with his nose tucked into a well-filled manger, and with nice dry bedding underneath him!

He looks round for a second, just to say, ' Well! I forgive you now for the misery of last night!'

I go out of the stable and back to the house, feeling that now Mrs. P—— will not spread her table in vain.

And, if these comforts for horse and man make so much difference—and I must honestly confess they do—what an additional pleasure it is when there is the sense of complete harmony in spiritual matters between host and guest. It is a thing to be thankful for, when on the following morning, as you are about to celebrate in the

Native Chapel close by, in comes the trader and kneels amongst his native customers.

You will say, perhaps, that this is a very glowing picture, and it all looks very *couleur de rose*, but you must not imagine that our friend P—— always lived as he does now, in the matter of worldly prosperity. I can well remember him when there was no Mrs. P——, no nice house, and no garden. In those days, a bit of a room separated off from his corrugated iron store was the extent of his 'house', and a very modest stipend the extent of his fortune.

Think of the common case of quite a boy being planted down in one of these very isolated trading stores. For five days of the week he sees no white man or woman. He spends all the day in his shop, listening to the talk—often very far from decent—of the Kafirs about him. In the evening he shuts up his store, makes up his books, and then what is there to do? It is, indeed, a heavy strain upon character, and the firm support of religion is the only thing which can uphold a man.

When Saturday comes, the doors are shut at one o'clock, and off goes the young trader, as fast as his pony can carry him, to the nearest European village. Supposing he is a stranger and has no friends, then he naturally turns in to the canteen, and the temptations of isolation amongst Kafirs are exchanged for temptations of a social kind amongst 'whites'.

But I did not mean when I began to write to say so much about the trader, and I must now turn to my real subject.

What is a trader's store? The difficulty I have is to say what it is not. I can hear many of my trader friends say, 'I can tell you what it is not. It is not a paying concern.'

I am not quite so sure about that. We can all see that competition has cut down profits in every direction, and the 'good old days' when an ox could be bought for a cotton blanket are, of course, gone for ever. But I still think that a comfortable income at any rate can be more easily earned in Kafir trading than in many a trade in the old country.

However, I am not now concerned with the profits, but with the 'store'. Outside, it certainly is not as a rule beautiful to look upon. But in spite of all the architectural glories of old England, I fear that we who cross the ocean must not throw too many stones. No corrugated iron store can be so much of a disfigurement to a landscape as the hideous advertisements which mar the pleasure of every journey in England.

Inside the store, a long counter runs down the middle, and behind this the shelves cover the walls, and are filled with the stock-in-hand of the trader.

In front of the counter is a railing dividing red-ochred from non-red-ochred customers. This is hardly a concession to superior pretensions on the part of the 'dressed' Kafirs, but a necessary protection both for the clothes of decent people and for the goods. Red-ochre is very tenacious stuff, which does not easily allow itself to be rubbed off. Frequently one sees dogs and even fowls emerging from a heathen kraal with absurdly pink 'complexions' from their contact with the blankets of their masters.

But still we are only at the beginning of our description of a trader's store.

The character of a man is not known by a description of his hat and clothes, and the Kafir store has a very real character which cannot be discovered by its outward appearance.

You may think that it exists solely for the purpose of buying and selling, but many a time I have been inclined to think—*pace* trader—that the mercantile element is a very subordinate one. Necessarily that side looms largely in the mind of the man behind the counter, whose patience must be sorely taxed by the demands made upon it.

I have gazed with admiration sometimes at the philosophical calmness with which some traders stand behind their counter at times when business is very brisk and customers impatient.

Tongues are all going at once, bare, red-ochred arms are eagerly gesticulating. Handkerchiefs full of eggs, buckets full of mealies, dishes of beans, are being thrust over the counter for sale. And all the time the trader quietly waits while some one decides between the merits of half a dozen 3*d*. coloured handkerchiefs! The handkerchief, when chosen, is done up in paper, the 3*d*. (tickey) is carefully unwrapped from a remote corner of the head scarf, a few sweets are given for an 'ibaso' ('extra' on the bargain), and the next customer gets a hearing.

But it cannot be expected that all traders should be alike endowed with such patience, and, indeed, the provocation at times must be very considerable. Occasionally a trader is known to adopt very forcible measures, but the moral authority of dignity and firmness is far more effectual than either loud shouting or violence.

How I should like to be able to take accurate snap-

shots with pen and ink of some of those many customers!
What sketches they would make for a traveller's note-
book!

Look at this old man who is just coming in. On his
head sits at an angle an old dilapidated ' billy-cock' hat,
on his back is something which was once a black frock
coat, while riding breeches, once white, with Wellington
boots, complete the costume.

Evidently he is a welcome customer, as at a sign from
the trader, way is at once made for him, and his wants
made known.

If you were to follow that old man home you would
soon see no more sign of the European clothes, and in
their place would appear the red blanket. He is an
uncle of the chief, and a headman, and holds himself
liable to the trader for all the purchases of those men of
his location who have no possessions as guarantee of
payment. He thus becomes responsible for two or three
hundred pounds made up of small sums ; but not one
does he forget. He remembers the man, the thing
purchased, and the amount. I remember once getting
that same old headman to sign (touch the pen while
I signed for him) a certain agreement about a school.
He then produced an old account book and asked me to
copy the agreement into that. Then he asked me
to read out various scarcely legible entries in his book,
and at each one he grunted his approval, and praised the
cleverness of his son who had learned to write.

The book, however, was quite unnecessary, as the old
man's memory for dealings was quite infallible. I should
add that he is not too great to spend ten minutes in
begging for a handful of tobacco.

Here comes in a very cheerful-looking young man, gathering his red-ochred blanket closely round him. Over his shoulder hangs a pair of boots, and he carries a parasol in his hand. He has just come back from the mines, with many gold pieces in his belt, and he is now going to settle the debts of his family.

Alas! sometimes the hard-earned savings of years are not brought back to the home. One particularly sad case was known to me. A Zulu, who had been working for several years at Kimberley and Johannesburg, came to the Mission to stay with friends, and there decided to marry and settle down. He was a good man, and a splendid worker, with arms like a blacksmith's, so I was glad to have him. He then told me that he had saved £80 from his earnings, and that he wanted to go up to Johannesburg to fetch this money. According to their custom he had distributed his savings amongst many friends, so that it would take some time to collect the whole sum. He collected it finally, and on the day before leaving the Transvaal he buried it for safety under a tree. Next morning the tree was there, but the money was gone. This is only one instance of several such cases I have known.

Let me point out one more customer only. Leaning over the counter at the far end you see a portly lady with a brilliant handkerchief round her head, and wearing a blanket much bedecked with beads. She is trying to catch the eye of the trader's assistant, and lifts an arm covered from wrist to elbow with bright brass bangles.

'My child,' she calls out, 'I am in a great hurry. When I left home the sun had not risen, and now it will be dark before I return.' She only comes from two miles off, and when she speaks it is eleven o'clock in the morning.

Again she calls out 'father' (sometimes even it is 'grandfather', although one minute ago it was 'child '), 'I am hungry, I have not yet eaten to-day, I must go home.'

Then, as the good-natured assistant turns to her, she says, 'Mhlekazi (O beautiful one), long have I waited, I want some salt for 3*d.*'

An hour later, you still see the same good lady begging some tobacco from some of her male friends outside the store. The pressing need of haste seems to be forgotten.

Very keen all these people are to get their money's worth. Each cotton blanket is held up to the light in turn, and no flaw escapes those quick eyes. The process of counting the change is a serious one amongst the wholly uneducated, and it is thought that two or three heads are better than one in such a matter. But, quick as they are, the Kafirs are sometimes strangely gullible. One afternoon I rode up to an isolated country store, and happened to notice outside a nice-looking ox, evidently brought for sale. That evening, the manager of the store asked me if I had seen this ox, and told me a curious story about it. He was very anxious to buy it, and offered the Kafir as much as £5 for it (a large price before the rinderpest). The owner refused, and stayed out all day expecting to get a higher bid. Late in the afternoon, the proprietor of the store rode up from elsewhere, and hearing the particulars from his manager, went outside to discuss the matter with the Kafir.

'Look here,' he said to him, 'what you want is calves,

is it not?' 'Yes,' answered the man. 'Three good calves would suit you well?' 'Yes.' 'Well, up at my place are some good calves at 30*s.*; here is £4 10*s.*, go up to-morrow and fetch your calves.'

The man left the ox, and went away satisfied.

Yes, day by day this sort of thing goes on, and yet it is undoubtedly true that buying and selling only form one part of the life-history of the Kafir store, and this is especially true of the isolated store in the country.

Hitherto I have spoken only of the business, but really busy hours when trade is brisk are comparatively few, and many an evening the trader must feel that, although his store has been used for a great many other purposes, trade has not been one of them.

If you will allow a certain width of meaning to my definitions, I should say that a Kafir store serves the following purposes :—

(1) General recreation room and music hall.

(2) Club for free inquiry.

(3) Debating room.

(4) Home for the weary.

(5) Bear-garden.

Now, my dear friend, don't get angry ; I did not say *your* store was all these things. I know what an excellent disciplinarian you are, and how you abhor rowdiness. Have you never said to me, 'No parson deserves to have a horse because he treats it so badly'? Of course, you go on to say, 'but you are an exception', and you send for your best horse and lend it to me for a fortnight. Well, we will say that you, too, are an exception, and we will cry peace. Bear with me at any rate while I venture to prove my words.

I have said in the first place that a trader's store is :—General recreation room and music hall.

I should say at the outset that smoking is *not* prohibited, and how it is that more stores are not burnt down is a matter of profound wonder to me. Smoking is not limited to one side of the counter, and the amount of matches and tobacco used yearly in the interior of all the Kafir stores in the Transkei would make an interesting calculation which I must leave to some of my friends in the business.

Nor is the music of a Kafir store entirely provided from one side of the counter alone. It is probable that the programme is never a fixed one, but the variety in some cases is quite surprising. At more than one store known to me, a gramophone carries to the ears of astonished Kafirs choice reproductions of London music halls. I should not like to say what the secret opinions of the hearers are about that instrument, but they shrug their shoulders and say 'Kwowk abelungu!' (Oh! these white men!).

> Behold in these, what leisure hours demand—
> Amusement and instruction hand in hand.

So runs the advertisement, but I venture to think those leisure hours could be better employed.

In another store I have seen a group of Kafirs sitting round a musical box, and behind many a counter is to be found a concertina, which is produced when business is slack, and when ears, wearied by the din of much conversation, need to be soothed by harmonious (?) sounds.

But the Kafirs contribute their share to the programme, although, unfortunately, it is not often that they use either their own primitive instruments or the good gifts of voice which they possess. Generally it is the mouth-organ, called by them 'piano', which is the underlying accompaniment of all the strange sounds of a Kafir store. Dancing, stimulated by the music, frequently takes place on the flat space of ground just outside. But I must not say more of the store as a music hall, so I will proceed to :—

(2) Club for free inquiry.

There is neither an entrance fee nor annual subscription to this club, nor is there a vote by ballot for membership. Even conditions of good behaviour are very easy. The inquiry may be very free indeed, but sometimes it is not quite so free as the response. It ranges from very terrestrial things, such as boot-laces, to very celestial things, such as the sun, the moon, and the stars. I believe *A Handy Traders' Encyclopedia* would have an enormous sale, but then the charms of complete freedom would be gone. Given an Encyclopedia the answer might be accurate, except, of course, in matters of Theology! And theological subjects are freely dealt with in the Kafir trading store.

Thirdly, I have described the store as a Debating room. The inquiries and the answers naturally lead sometimes to discussion, and discussion develops into debate. For the moment trade is suspended, the trader sits up on the counter, lights his pipe, and either takes a leading part or else sums up the debate at the end.

I remember on one occasion being the unconscious means of starting such a debate on a small scale.

I had only been out in the country a year, and I happened to walk into a Kafir store in a very out-of-the-way place. I went in, and shook hands with the

trader—a Scotchman whom I knew—and nodded to
some Kafirs who were making purchases. Suddenly
one of them—a man dressed in black—turned to the
trader and, pointing to me, said in good English—'You
see this Umfundisi who comes into your store. He is
too proud to notice me now. But once he came to my
house when he was ill. I took him in, gave him food,
and rubbed his back with paraffin oil. Now he will not
notice me.' Before I could say a word, the Scotchman,
knowing nothing of the circumstances, took up the
cudgels on my behalf, and a regular debate began.
I must confess I was not satisfied with the line of defence
adopted by my 'counsel'. He reminded this man, who
appeared to be a Wesleyan minister, of the sermon he
had preached on the Sermon on the Mount about giving
and not expecting a reward, about forgiving enemies,
&c., &c. The trader's eloquence was all in vain; the
Wesleyan minister was quite implacable. At last I was
allowed to explain, and I succeeded in partly convincing
the offended minister that I had not been guilty of
intentional discourtesy.

On the occasion when he was kind enough to take
me in, I had been two weeks in the country, and
could no more distinguish one individual from another
amongst the Kafirs than one sheep from another in a
flock.

Then, fourthly, the trader's store is a Home for the
weary. When I add this to the purposes of a store,
I am not primarily thinking of the Kafirs. I have no
doubt that some of those women who have tramped for
miles and miles with heavy loads of firewood or baskets
of grain on their heads are remarkably thankful to arrive

at their destination, and do find it a home for the weary.
But I was thinking rather of weary missionaries, who so
often owe a debt of gratitude to the trader, not only for
liberal hospitality, but also for a bed on his counter.
There is quite a fascinating excitement about a night on
the top of a tall counter. Personally I am an undis-
ciplined person in my sleep, and go off to sleep with
a very considerable apprehension about the drop of three
and a half feet on either side. Frequently when I wake
up I find myself feeling the counter to measure my
distance from the edge. In course of time I think the
risk of a fall would act as a good sedative.

Again, the store is—(5) 'A bear-garden'.

I will most gladly say that this term cannot be applied
without making many exceptions. Nevertheless it is the
only word I can think of which will at all fit certain
scenes I have occasionally witnessed.

Quite probably the majority of those people who
behaved themselves so riotously had come straight from
a 'beer-drink'. Outside the shop the young men are
fencing, while the girls stand about shouting, laughing,
and dancing. Inside, the whole available space is filled,
and the noise is absolutely deafening. The atmosphere
reeks of Kafir beer and pungent smoke, and the wild
excited looks of men and women dwell unpleasantly in
one's memory.

Such, briefly, is the Kafir store, and I feel that I have
scarcely done justice to its many-sidedness.

I will again say that the influences passing over that
counter can hardly be exaggerated. Every day is potent
in a hundred directions for good or evil. Those scales,
which occupy so prominent a place on the counter, are

not nearly as important as the mental scales in which
English character is being weighed.

If Christ were acknowledged in word and life in every
trader's store, the results would be immeasurable. I am
thankful to say, in spite of many failures (and missionaries
fail as well as traders), there is much to be thankful for.

When one trader sits up night after night with a dying
Christian native ; when another supports a boy at the
Mission School, who could not otherwise be supported ;
when another works with his own hands to build the
native church,—with evidences such as these, who will
say that trade is altogether in the opposite camp to
missionary enterprise?

CHAPTER III

STORM-RESISTING AND STORM-COMPELLING

THERE are times in South Africa when climate and soil seem to conspire together to show what they can do. At such times a ride through the ploughing lands is a great delight. The tall graceful stalks of the mealie plant and the full-grained red heads of the Kafir corn rise up above you on either side. Enormous pumpkins peep out from their half-hidden bed below. The valleys seem to 'laugh and sing'. Yet even at that stage anxiety is not at an end. After a few hours only you may return from your ride to find in the place of that smiling plenty, a strange scene of desolation.

Over the far-off summits of the Drakensberg Mountains, a few white clouds make their appearance in the blue sky. Very innocent of evil they look at ten o'clock in the morning, but experienced people already shake their heads.

By one o'clock those clouds are no longer in their initial stage of harmlessness, and even the trustful begin to suspect their intentions. Magnificent they are while the sun still shines upon their noble outlines, but behind the brilliant white are gathering shades of black. At two o'clock the sun has been overtaken, and now it is too late to send out messengers to ask 'Is it peace?' A low muffled growl is the answer to our ultimatum. War is declared, and from the rapidly advancing army, first one

huge Goliath and then another steps forward to terrify
the hearts of the fearful.

Out rushes the David of heathen life, armed, not with
trust in the living God, but with the magic arts of witchcraft. Fearfully he curses the approaching enemies.
Wilder and wilder become his gesticulations. In vain
is the fight between such unequal foes. The clouds now
close together, and present a serried mass—the lightning
dazzles with its fierce light, the thunder bursts out as
if from a few feet overhead, and then rolls away with
heavy rumblings into distance. Between the peals of
thunder is heard a curious, steady, distant roar as of the
heavy tramp of an approaching army. A few big drops
fall one by one, and then down the rain comes in an
irresistible torrent. But, behind the rain, and louder
than the splash of water, is that strange roar of the
dreaded enemy. On it comes, nearer and nearer, until
despair is written upon every face. The jagged lumps
of ice now come pouring down with a terrific deafening
noise. A short fifteen minutes, and it is all over. The
heavy clouds roll away until they are only seen as
a distant purple bank, from out of which are heard
occasional sounds of low muffled thunder. The blue
sky appears, and the sun shines out, but the faces of
men do not respond. There is a dazzling brightness
in the air, and the sides of the mountain glisten as the
sun catches the waves of falling water and the fields of
melting ice.

But the hearts of men are heavy as they still sit
crouching over the fires in their huts.

At last, one by one, they slink out as men who have
escaped from the awful carnage of a battlefield. Why

have they such a strange, guilty look as they turn their
eyes towards the ploughing lands ?   Is it that they would
like to curse, but dare not ?   Is it that they are afraid of
that angry, resentful feeling which springs up in their
hearts ?   Is it that a sudden quick thought reminds them
that the weapons of those dread malevolent powers are
still ready?

Grievous indeed is the sight which now meets the eye.
I have seen the ravages of locusts, and the cruel grip of
an early frost upon the yet tender grain, but for desolation, nothing that I know of quite comes up to the
after-path of a severe hail-storm. Where, in the morning,
you looked upon fields of luxurious growth, you see now
the bare earth furrowed in all directions by the rapid
rush of waters.

Down those newly made streams all the produce of
those fields has been carried to the rivers.   Green-brown
stalks, with floating ribands, alone remain to testify to
the industry and hopes of a year.

On the following day many a Kafir may be seen
trudging along the road which leads to the railway and
to the mines. They chat, they laugh, and they smoke
as though nothing unusual had happened. In that particular locality the witch doctor was overcome, but in
other and more fortunate places he holds his head an
inch higher.

The Kafir does not complain of his misfortune, and
the mine-owner is glad.

Hail is a deadly foe, but its ravages are generally con-
fined in area to a narrow strip of country. Those who lose
their all will, at any rate, have no difficulty in buying
from their more favoured neighbours. A more deadly,

because a more universal, enemy is the drought. Storm-compelling, or rain-making, is consequently even more important than storm-resisting.

This branch of public service used to be entirely in the hands of the chiefs themselves, but now it appears to be open to all competitors. Sir Harry Smith, in his *Autobiography*, tells an amusing story of his efforts to stamp out belief in the rain-doctors in South Africa. He says:—' One day when the great rain-maker was in my camp, and many others, as well as an unusually large number of Kafirs, I assembled them all for the avowed purpose of hearing a disputation between the " Great Chief " or " Father ", as they invariably called me, and the rain-makers. My first question to them was, " So you can make rain, can you ? "

' I never saw in men's countenances more caution. I said, " Speak out, speak freely to your Father." The great rain-maker said he could. I then showed him one by one all the articles on my writing-table, knives, scissors, &c., my clothes, my hat, boots, &c., asking, " Can you make this ? " " No." " Do you know how it is made ? " " No." Having explained everything, and how it was made, through the medium of my invaluable interpreter, Mr. Shepstone, I then called for a tumbler of water. I showed all the people the water, and asked the rain-makers if what was in the glass was of the same quality as the water or rain they invoked. All agreed " Yes." Their anxiety was intense. I then threw down the water on the dry ground, which immediately absorbed it, and desired the rain-makers to put it again in the tumbler. They were aghast and said, " We cannot." In a voice of thunder I said, " Put the rain again in this

glass, I say." I then turned to the spectators, " Now
you see how these impostors have deceived you. Now
listen to the 'Word'." (This is the phrase they use
in giving orders and decisions on all points of law and
in trials.) I took my wand of office, planted it violently
before me and said, "Any man of my children hereafter
who believes in witchcraft, or that any but God the
Great Spirit can make rain, I will ' eat him up '." I then
left the meeting and the rain-makers thunderstruck and
confounded.'

One cannot help applauding Sir Harry Smith for his
intentions and his confidence ; but if he had known the
Kafirs rather better he would neither have adopted such
a method nor have believed in its success. It is fortunate
perhaps that he could not read the thoughts of the
' thunderstruck and confounded' rain-makers. Light
and darkness must still have a long struggle before the
belief in rain-making by witchcraft dies away. Amongst
the Pondomisi the great rain-doctor is a little old bushman. He is the sole survivor in that part of the country
of an almost extinct people. It is always said the present
chief of the Pondomisi has a strain of bushman blood in
him, and both he and his people are proud of being
called the children of the bushwoman.

It appears that an ancient Pondomisi chief married
a bushwoman among other wives, and by her skill in
cookery she became the chief wife. She had a method
of mincing the meat and cooking it with fat which made
it very soft and palatable. Bishop Key says of this
legend : ' This story exemplifies again the ups and downs
of the polygamic family, and the fortunes of its members.
An industrious woman may, it is well known, make her

house a strong and important one, even though by right it is of inferior order, by the care with which she prepares the food. By attention to its quality and quantity, she attracts adherents who will flock to her house when they come to "busa", i. e., serve at the great place, knowing that they will find plenty reigning there instead of starvation. All the food supply is under the control of the lady of the house. The gardens are called by her name and cannot be encroached upon by her sister wives. And though the men generally give their aid in the cultivation, they go as assistants, they will tell you, to Ma-so-and-so's garden. The more adherents she can gather, the larger the land cultivated, and the more certain is the crop.

'Where a woman, from her industry or other good qualities, is a general favourite, her house becomes rich in peace and powerful in war.

'Doubtless the success of the bushwoman was due to something of this nature, for it is hardly consistent with Kafir custom to suppose that she was formally made the great wife from her skill in culinary art . . .'

The bushmen have left many a trace of their existence and of their skill, in the curious paintings which adorn the sides and roofs of the caves formerly occupied by them. They must have had knowledge of some good pigments, as well as the aptitude to use them.

I have seen quaint representations of battles between themselves armed with bow and arrow (poisoned) and the Kafirs armed with shield and assegais. Hunting scenes are also common. They seem to have been a very nomadic people, living solely by their skill as hunters. They are extremely small in stature, with a brownish yellow skin, high protruding cheek-bones, and sharp, cunning eyes. The sole survivor of pure bushman blood in these parts is now the accredited rain-doctor to the Pondomisi, and taxes their credulity for his living.

The temptation to turn to any ' Pied Piper ' who can promise to compel the clouds with his music, must be a very great one.

An Englishman who has never left his own country, can have little conception of the effects of a South African drought. During the winter, from April to September, rain is not expected, and the whole country dries up to a russet-brown. Broad stretches of the veld are now burnt off, and the black, parched ground eagerly awaits the first rains of spring. The cattle wander from one spot to another in search of some pasture which will at least maintain life. There is a general feeling of expectation in the air. The mountains, the veld, the springs, the animals, and all the tribes of man seem to be waiting for a great benefactor to appear. No date has been fixed, but his visit has been long deferred. All eyes turn furtively to the road along which he is to travel. A sense of unsettlement reigns through the country. When day follows day, and still rain does not come, the sense of disappointed expectation changes to that of unfulfilled claim. The people feel like hungry men who have been invited to a feast where there is no food. Their host is like one ' who boasteth himself of a false gift ', and the author of the Book of Proverbs tells us that such a man is ' like clouds and wind without rain '. Cold has given place to heat, the veld has been

burnt off, the ploughs are all ready. But in vain keen
ears listen for the splashing of the drops. The strangest
feature of the drought is that each day dawns bright
with hope. The sun grows fiercer and fiercer, black
clouds gather, thunder crashes out with short, hard notes.
The lightning-flashes are more and more vivid and intense. But there is no rain, and ' Hope deferred maketh
the heart sick '.

October and November have both passed, and with
them all hope of ploughing has nearly vanished. In
December the days lengthen, and the heat in-
creases. The cattle lie down in the kraal at night,
and in the morning have no strength to rise up without
help.

The strong survive, but woe to the weak among the
flocks. There is no soft feeling of pity in the savage
crows—they wait until the poor sheep have no more
strength to resist, but they do not wait until life has
passed away. Outside the trader's store are rows upon
rows of hides, and by the sale of these the Kafir can still
smoke his pipe and wait.

> No! penury, inertness and grimace
> In some strange sort, were the land's portion. ' See
> Or shut your eyes,' said Nature peevishly,
> It nothing skills: I cannot help my case:
> 'Tis the Last Judgement's fire must cure this place,
> Calcine its clods and set my prisoners free.
> Byron's *Childe Roland to the Dark Tower came.*

And what is our friend the bushman doing all this
time? Why does he not rescue the people from their
misery? Messengers go to inquire the reasons for this
strange neglect of duty. They return to say that no

INTERIOR OF OLD CHURCH—S. CUTHBERT'S.

To face page 31.

rain can be given until an ox with very peculiar marks
is procured. When this has been found and sent, the
blame is laid upon the sorcery of some supposed enemy.
So it goes on from day to day until appearances are
more favourable. . . . At last the heavens relent, and
there is a sweet sound of falling drops. No music in the
world could be quite so welcome to the ear and heart.
Now the rain comes down until the hot, parched earth
yields a fragrant scent, and the poor tired leaves on the
trees once more lift up their heads.

The tension is passed; and although the results of the
drought cannot be at once removed, the faces of men
respond to the change about them. Gradually the
whole country begins to smile. Carpets of green are
lightly thrown over the black pall left by the fire.
Flowers spring out of the short grass, adding to it
touches of brilliant colour. From dawn until late at
night the ploughs are at work, using each precious
minute.

In course of time both drought and rain alike seem to
be forgotten. Grain is again plentiful, the cattle are
once more fat and strong. Every morning the smoke
from some distant kraal speaks of Kafir beer and meat.
The bushman again receives his taxes for benefits past
or future.

Are there a few who do not forget? Are there not
some who remember the days of evil and the lessons
of penitence? Were there not any who said 'God
withholds the good in order that we may prize the
better'?

Day by day in front of the Altar of a little Mission
Church we see the first-fruits of the crop—mealies, pump-

kins, beans, and sugar-cane. What do these offerings mean? Do they not mean that throughout all that time of anxiety and suffering, some hearts were brave, some there were whose faith did not waver, some who believed still that God is love, some who asked to learn the lesson of His visitation?

CHAPTER IV

NOMLALA AND HIS SONS

I HAVE very often felt that one of the great dangers in missionary work of to-day is that we are unable to get into sufficiently close touch with the heathen people.

Other claims upon the missionary are so numerous— 'the children must first be fed', and there are white children as well as black.

In many parishes the number of native Christians runs into four figures, and their needs are felt to be so pressing that the claims of the heathen fall into the background. Native preachers go out amongst them to 'compel them to come in', but we ourselves do not reach them. The loss is bound to be a great one. We go out primarily to fulfil and not to destroy, and a personal knowledge of the moral consciousness of the heathen must be very important. We need to sound their moral and religious instincts, as a doctor sounds his patients with his stethoscope. We are looking for the 'Altar to the unknown God' which is built up somewhere in every human heart. We dig for it underneath all the surface appearances of indifference, because upon it we want to see the sacrifice of prayer ascending to God, who has revealed Himself in Jesus Christ.

We may not expect to find much positive religion. The 'Unkulunkulu' of heathen thought may very possibly be only a sort of a deified ancestral chief. We may find more and more that the one desire of the heathen mind is not to formulate a belief in the unseen, but rather to hide from it. It may seem that it is impossible to give the name 'religion' to that which seeks to escape fellowship. But yet, in moral instincts which are at the root of all that is good in social life; in the sense of loyalty to their chief; in the honour which responds to trust; in the charity which is generous to the needy; in the affections which bind together the home, we find some stones of that altar. Him therefore, whom they worship in ignorance, it is our privilege to proclaim.

But all this requires much continuous personal intercourse with the heathen, and this is what we have been unable to accomplish. I often felt the loss of this intercourse when I saw Bishop Key chatting with some veterans of the old Pondomisi tribe. He seemed to know them so intimately, and to call out the best in them. He never looked so happy as when a few of these men were lounging about him in their red-ochred blankets. One old man, Ncotane, was one of the Bishop's particular favourites. I fancy, during some war Ncotane had been obliged to hide for his life in the forest, and had sent word of his plight to Bishop Key. The Bishop had sent him a horse, upon which he managed to effect his escape, but the form of his gratitude was characteristically Kafir. The Kafir, when he thanks you, kisses your hand and then says either 'Nangomso' (Again to-morrow!) or else 'Mus' ukudinwa' (Don't get tired!). Whenever Bishop Key was in the neighbourhood of S. Cuthbert's, old Ncotane used to hear of it, and he invariably wound up a pleasant chat with an appeal to the Bishop's heart.

I used sometimes to regret that it had not been part

of my experience to settle down for a time amongst the heathen, unhampered by the claims of a large and growing work. In those early days when Bishop Key first settled on the banks of the Inxu river, he could attempt little more than to win the friendship and confidence of the people. For any conversions he had to be content to wait, and to realize that he was sowing seed which some day would take root downwards and spring upwards.

One of the first converts to Christianity, if not actually the first, from the Pondomisi tribe was a Nomlala, and the stipulation he made was very characteristic. He said he was a man 'who loved the enemies', and that when he became a Christian he ought to be allowed to go out to war. Certainly he would not have been a true son of his father if he had not 'loved the enemies', for old Nomlala seems to have been a great warrior. On one occasion he valiantly rescued the old chief Diko when he was wounded, and about to fall into the hands of the foes. But old Nomlala was evidently a cunning councillor as well as a warrior. Bishop Key tells the following story of him in his history of the Pondomisi :—

' The Government had sent Colonel Somerset to recover cattle stolen by the Gaikas. . . . Diko, the chief of the Pondomisi, appears to have sent messengers to the officer in command, who received them kindly and invited all friends of the English to join in their cause.

' Soon Hintsa, the paramount chief of all the Xosa tribes, came into the camp to treat in person. He was made a sort of prisoner or hostage for the surrender of the cattle, and when Diko sent another embassy, Nomlala, who was one of the messengers, asked a very pertinent

question—a question which exemplifies the cautious
Kafir character:—

' " Now that the chief is in the hands of the white men,
and we are taking messages to the white chief, supposing
something happened to him (Hintsa), shall not we be
guilty ? " There was no answer to the shrewd question,
and the men went back.'

Nomlala's instinct on this occasion made him a true
prophet, as Hintsa attempted to escape from the English
and was shot.

The Pondomisi were never a military people like the
Zulus under Tshaka, or some other tribes which imitated
them. Tshaka must have been a military genius, and,
as he was never deterred by the slightest feelings of
humanity or pity, his reign was a long carnival of bloodshed. His soldiers were separated into regiments distinguished by different coloured shields, and they were
trained under the fierce discipline of an autocrat who
regarded killing as a pastime. Failure in warfare was
punished by Tshaka with immediate death.

The Pondomisi had no such thirst for war, and if left
alone by their enemies, would speedily have settled
down into a quiet pastoral people. They might occasionally have made depredations upon their neighbour's
cattle kraals, but warfare would never have been their
main occupation. In those days, however, a tribe must
either fight or become a prey to other tribes, and very
seldom a year passed without the war-cry. The thoughts
of the men must have continually been turned to the
excitements of hunting, and to the glories of battle. The
one ambition of the youths of the nation must have
been to emulate the deeds of some of their heroes.

We must expect a certain 'drop' in turning from the records of these stirring days to the quieter times of Government protection, when the swords are turned into plowshares, and the spears into pruning-hooks.

If we were reading the lives of some of the heroes of Ladysmith, we should perhaps feel a similar 'drop', when, after all the thrilling records of that siege, we read of our heroes leaving South Africa and returning to the humdrum life of an English town. We do not feel the same interest in the wall-paper and the furniture as we did in the trenches and shelters. The sounds of the traffic in the streets and the cries of the newspaper boys do not excite us as did the whistle of the bullet and the bark of the pom-poms.

And yet, if we have eyes to see it, there is a warfare of greater importance and of more real interest going on in each individual life. It may be hidden or obscured by all the circumstances of daily life, but there is a story to be read, sometimes of defeat, of surrender, or of compromise, and sometimes of courage, of victory, and of great reward. It is of that warfare that I want to write now.

It may be that often we cannot see beyond our own individual conflict, but here and there we come near to one another as 'ships that pass in the night', and we catch glimpses of that inner warfare which determines the outward life.

I do not profess to be qualified to give a full account of the Nomlala family. To do this I should need to gain much more information than I now possess from those competent to give it. But I have had intimate acquaintance with several members of the family for some years, and I think there is a good deal in my recollections of them which may be of interest.

I have not chosen to speak of the Nomlalas because they have been foremost in maintaining Christianity, but rather because their family strikingly illustrates the warfare ever going on between light and darkness. The message of Christ certainly brought them a sword and not peace. When the acceptance of Christianity is very definite, it often happens that the sword is soon sheathed because opposition soon dies away.

But where there is the tendency to compromise, the divisions may be less acute, but they are more lasting. How well we know this amongst ourselves!

I always felt that there was this note of compromise about the Christianity in the Nomlala family, and that this accounted for the long endurance of the heathen element.

I have known four sons of old Nomlala, but I do not expect that they were all the children of the same mother. Two of the four sons are alive, and remain heathen, the other two were both Christians, and have passed away.

Of the two former I have not very much to say. The eldest son, Nqwashu, is now an old man, and is no longer able to carry on the duties of a Government headman, in which capacity I have always known him. I always felt that life must have become rather a complicated and puzzling matter to this old man.

He is essentially one of the old Kafirs who belong to a past generation. For him, a good deal of the interest and romance of life must have departed with the abolition of war and hunting.

As I have sat talking in meetings with him and his

men, I have often wished I could get inside the old man's mind for a few minutes, and see things with his eyes. I have wondered how far he discerns the true proportions of the great change which has taken place in his lifetime.

Apart altogether from the excitements of war and the chase, so much that is good has gone, and is going, out of Kafir life. The axes and hammers of modern civilization have been at work upon the real monuments of the past.

How much does old Nqwashu see? Does he see at all? If he does see, I have a great sympathy for him, because I feel quite sure that he does not also see the full measure of the compensations. Doubtless he perceives the surface changes in Kafir life, and I think that the sight must bring with it a touch of cynicism. It is not hard to become a cynic where white meets black, where civilization meets the 'primitive order', where Christianity meets heathenism. It does not need a Gibbon to expose the inconsistencies, and to smile at exaggerations. I fear that Nqwashu, in moments of reflection, must often have occasion to see that European clothing does not always go hand in hand with loyalty, manliness, and courage; that prayers and hymns are not always associated with the Christian virtues.

Perhaps, however, he is content not to think at all. The new order is altogether too much of a puzzle. In the old days his intellect was a match for any man's. At that time the criminal was exposed by a process of masterly cross-questioning in the presence of the chief. In this art Nqwashu was supreme. But now, intellects, like assegais, grow rusty.

The magistrate's court has largely taken the place of the chief's kraal.

Written books have taken the place of good memories. White law agents are now hired to contend that the criminal is not guilty, while men of keen intellect sit by silent.

Well—it is all a great puzzle to old Nqwashu. He sees a good deal, and what he sees, he does not altogether like. There is also a good deal that he cannot see, and much of that is good.

So Nqwashu has put himself on the shelf, and a younger man is now 'headman' of the Xabane in his place.

Now we come to the next son, Nqandeka, and his history is a very remarkable one.

In the case of Nqwashu, the eldest son, the transformation of Kafir life has been a gradual one. He has seen the changes step by step. But Nqandeka has, by a very curious experience, failed to be a witness of all the intervening stages of the transformation.

Just after tribal rule was supplanted by Government administration, he left Kafir-land with his mind only charged, as it were, with memories of the past, and he returned to it two years ago to find the pictures of his memory gone, and the new order fully established.

Twenty years or more ago Nqandeka was convicted of murder by the English magistrate at Qumbu. The case was a complicated one, and others besides himself were implicated. However, he was sentenced, I believe, to the breakwater at Capetown for life. If he had been judged a few years previously by his own chief, matters would have been very different. He would not have

KAFIR WOMAN (HEATHEN) STAMPING MEALIES, WITH CHRISTIAN
WOMAN AND CHILDREN ON THE RIGHT.

To face page 41.

stood before the chief as an individual merely, but as the member of a family. The whole Nomlala family would have fathered him, and would have stepped forward at the conclusion of the trial to pay the allotted fine of oxen.

When I arrived at the Mission, Nqandeka had already served some years as a convict. He left behind him a wife and some children, but the only one of the family whom I really knew very well was the second son, who had become a Christian, and had received the name of Wellington.

After passing out of the ordinary school, Wellington had gone into the carpenter's shop, and although he was not very quick, he acquired a very good knowledge of his trade. Latterly he was frequently employed by Europeans at a wage of five shillings a day, and he was also greatly in demand amongst the natives for jobs in their huts, and for making tables, chairs, &c.

In character he was weak, and gave us a good deal of anxiety, but a few years ago he married a good Christian girl, and settled down very happily at a place a few miles distant from the Mission.

I can so well recall my last visit to Wellington and Agnes in their new home. I was riding past their kraal early one morning on my way to visit a dying man, and Wellington came out and asked me to stop and see them on my way back.

On my return I found that Agnes had boiled a kettle of water and was making some tea for me. They only had two huts, one small one for a kitchen, and a larger one in which we sat. Wellington's trade had been most useful to him in setting up a house for himself, and I looked with pleasure at the various things he had made.

Often and often Wellington had come to me to ask if nothing could be done to set his father free. Both Bishop Key and I had carefully gone into the case, and had sent more than one petition to the Government, but without success. Occasionally Nqandeka would get some one to write for him to Wellington, telling him that some more fortunate companion had been 'pardoned', and urging him to do more for him. In these letters he always asked affectionately after his wife and family.

I had quite given up all hope of ever hearing of his release, when suddenly, about three years ago, news arrived that he was to be set free. Alas! it was too late for his wife, who had died just before he arrived.

And now we come to a singular episode in the story. Naturally I had hoped that Nqandeka would settle down with his son Wellington, and would become a Christian. Presently, to my surprise, I heard that immediately after his arrival, a strange misunderstanding had arisen between Nqandeka and his son Wellington. The origin of this misunderstanding, although full of interest, is too long to be detailed here. I am afraid one of the chief reasons for it was that the wife of Wellington's choice was not to the mind of the rest of the family, and Nqandeka did not espouse his son's cause.

There was another reason which was always being hinted at, but of which they would not speak openly before me. I believe it was that Wellington had chosen for his new home the neighbourhood of the place where the murder in which his father was implicated had been committed.

I did my best to act as peacemaker in the matter, but did not succeed very well.

There was something so sad in the return of this old man to his home, after serving twenty years or more as a convict, to find his wife dead and his son—to his thinking —unfilial.

But the saddest part of the story is yet to come. Wellington was suddenly taken ill, and after receiving the last sacraments of the Church, died, leaving poor Agnes a widow, and his father with a sore heart.

I must now leave the story of Nqandeka, and turn to the other two sons of old Nomlala, who were both Christians.

I imagine it was Mengqupo, the elder, who reminded Bishop Key that he was a man 'who loved the enemies'.

I think sometimes that I used to be rather hard in my judgement of old Mengqupo, and that I did not make enough allowances for him. There was a certain proud distinction in being the first convert from among the Pondomisi, and also a singular friend of Bishop Key. I can quite imagine that he would feel himself to be entitled to exceptional indulgence on this account. Then, too, even in the Church, things had changed, and, with the growth of the work, new discipline had become necessary, and many customs formerly allowable had become forbidden to Christians.

When I got to know him better, I became very much attached to him, and it was quite a proud moment when one day old Mengqupo suddenly turned upon me with a glowing face, and said, 'We see to-day that you have the heart of Bishop Key.'

According to his lights, I believe old Mengqupo to
have lived and died a loyal Christian, but in his latter
years the poor old man had sore troubles in his family.

Amongst ourselves we are often astonished at the
strange contrasts to be found in sons of the same parents,
and brought up under exactly the same conditions. I
suppose it is easier to understand such contrasts amongst
a people in the transition stage between heathenism and
Christianity ; but it was a remarkably wide gulf which
separated Qikani and Robert, two of the sons of Mengqupo. Both were, I believe, baptized as children, but
eventually Qikani, the elder, ' lapsed ' from all practice
of Christianity, married two wives, and actually became
a witch-doctor.

The profession of a witch-doctor implies a very considerable amount of degradation in a man who has been
at least confronted with Christian ideals. It is true, as
Mr. Kidd points out, that a witch-doctor is not the same
as a sorcerer, who uses magic for private ends. As a
matter of fact, one great work of the witch-doctor is to
protect society from the magic of the sorcerers. But
the whole process of initiation and the sense of trading
upon the delusions of the people, must be terribly
demoralizing.

There was something so very horrible in the thought
of this poor man who had once been made a member of
Christ by baptism, now professing communion with
demons. Dressed up in the usual costume of wild skins,
with a fur cap on his head, he would dance himself into
the frenzied state in which the spirits are supposed to
speak to him. Then would follow the cunning system of
questioning the people who come to him, in order to

discover the object of their visit. The people answer by
clapping their hands and shouting ' Siyavuma ' (We agree),
and by the degree of enthusiasm in their response, the
witch-doctor knows if he is on the right track. Fortunately the last step in this weird performance cannot now
be put into practice. The Government has put down
with a strong hand ' the smelling-out ', by which the
supposed enemy or sorcerer was driven from home, his
possessions robbed, and himself sometimes killed.

It is a pleasant relief to turn from Qikani to his brother.
Robert was a quiet unassuming fellow, who became quite
one of our best teachers, and was much loved both by his
school children and their parents. It was a real pleasure
to go into his school and see the neat, methodical way
in which he carried on his work. After he had been
teaching for a short time he began to look forward to
marriage, but chest troubles set in, and after a very short
illness Robert, who was the joy of his old father's heart,
was taken away.

I have spoken briefly of three sons of old Nomlala and
of their families. I now come to Mawela (or Albert, as
he was baptized), the son with whom I was most intimate.
I must confess that Mawela was not always an exem-
plary Christian, and that at times he was responsible for
a great deal of trouble and unhappiness on the Mission.
Nevertheless, my heart warms as I think of him, and
as I remember the happy way in which his life was
ended.

What a merciful thing it is that when a man has gone
away out of mortal sight, we instinctively turn away from
the clouds and shadows of his life. We think of the man
as a whole, of what he was developing into, and we

rejoice to know that the real man was the man in his moments of penitence. It is in repentance that we disown the untrue self and own the true.

I have known Mawela at his worst, but I am thankful to say I have also known him at his best. I have seen him when all the meaner characteristics of Kafir character seemed alone to be evident, and I have seen him when I have delighted in his greatness. Are there not some people and some circumstances which always bring out the mean and shabby in us, just as there are other people and other circumstances which bring out the best?

I do not think we make enough allowance for this when we are presented with a double picture of the Christian Kafir. The two pictures are frequently so very opposite, although one gratefully recognizes the growing tendency of the more attractive one to dominate the other, and to produce a better and higher combination in the end.

The ordinary traders' estimate of the Christian Kafir, which figures so often in the records of the hasty traveller, is so different from that of the enthusiastic missionary.

I will venture to claim that the trader is generally far more one-sided, and less qualified to form a true judgement than the missionary. But in any case, the difference between them is sufficiently startling, and after all deductions have been made to allow for the 'point of view' of the respective critics, the pictures refuse to harmonize.

Now, do not let us try to account for this by saying that the missionary is a good truthful person, and the trader is not. Nor let us say that the missionary wants to see the good, and the trader does not. I am thankful to say I know many traders of the highest character, for whom I have a profound respect, and I am sure they want to see good, and not evil, and rejoice when they can see it.

Now I am quite certain that I could pick out a certain number of our Christian natives of whom these traders would approve as absolutely as myself. I think I could also pick out some of whom I should disapprove as emphatically as do my friends the traders, although, perhaps, I should make more allowances, and take a more hopeful view. It seems to me that it is about the inter-mediate mass of people that our verdicts might differ— those who are neither very definitely good nor very definitely bad.

Many things can be said to account to some extent for this difference. Of these I will not speak, nor will I venture to ask who is the better judge.

But surely we do often forget to make sufficient allowance for the circumstances under which we respec-tively see the same people. Of course the truly consis-tent man is ever the same in character, whether he is in his home, or whether he is in his shop ; whether he is alone in his room, or whether he is in society ; whether he is at Ascot, or whether he is taking the chair at a temperance lecture.

But without being hypocrites, we are not all of us equally consistent. I do not mean to say that we put on our religion and take it off as we do our greatcoat ; but we are quite conscious that all that is good and religious in us springs up in response to certain surroundings, and to the influence of certain people, while all that is worldly and frivolous in us comes to the front on other occasions. More particularly is this the case with emotional people, who are often in sore perplexity over this strange readiness in themselves to respond freely and quickly to apparently contradictory influences.

Now, the Kafirs are an emotional people, and I do not think we allow enough for this readiness to be different at different times, yet without being hypocrites.

Take one small point as an illustration. The Kafir as I have known him is avaricious and covetous. In some ways he is a trader born. He may make many stupid mistakes about his dealings, but his one aim always has been, and always will be, to make a bargain. He will cheerfully walk twenty miles to a shop, if he thinks that he can buy a blanket twopence cheaper there than at his own door.

Nor is it to be expected that he will have a very high sense of truthfulness in his commercial dealings. (I am speaking not of Christian or heathen as such, but of the typical Kafir.) He will generally be as truthful as the other man expects him to be, and the other man generally expects very little. He would probably take rather a high view of the requirements of truth when speaking to a chief; but a very, very low view when engaged in commercial dealings. Unfortunately, too, his experience of European standards of commercial honour has not always helped him to take a higher view. The European standard may not be ideally Christian in Europe, and in some ways it tends to come down in Kafir-land.

The Kafir would find it difficult to draw the same distinctions which have become customary to some of us. He knows that when he is hard pressed, and goes

NOMLALA AND HIS SONS

to the trader to borrow money, he does it at the cost
of sixty per cent. Often, too, he (very foolishly) sells his
grain at the beginning of the year for 8s. per sack, and
has to buy it back at the end for 30s. He would find it
very puzzling to be told that by the same standard he is
a dishonest man for saying that his cow is a paragon,
and worth £20, when as a matter of fact she has ceased
to calve.

My point is this. In commercial dealings you touch
the Kafir at his weakest point, and you must not judge
him too hardly. Because you find him displaying un-
christian qualities over the counter, or because some of
his practices there cannot be brought into strict harmony
with the ' code ', which is to some extent artificial, do not
be too ready to say that he is a hypocrite for reading the
Bible and going to church.

It may seem that I have got far away from Mawela
Nomlala, but I have not really done so, for in all this
discussion I have had my mind fixed upon him, and he
has furnished my text.

I always felt when I had any commercial dealings with
him, that I could understand the trader's point of view in
his estimate of the Christian Kafir. But I could always
see the other side of Mawela's character, and I knew he
was no hypocrite. In striking a bargain he was a typical
Kafir, and, so long as I treated him as the typical Kafir,
I knew he would hold out for the longest price, and
would employ the extremest art of the professional
bargainer.

When I refused to deal with him as the typical Kafir,
and made him realize that, even in selling his forage or
his beans, he was a Christian, Mawela was a different

person. As a 'dealer', I did not like Mawela, but as a man, I loved him. I can think now of certain occasions when I have taken a positive delight in him. As a 'councillor' he was admirable. He knew all the ins and outs of Kafir custom, and had a wonderful faculty for turning an intricate case inside out. I often gave him work to do which required keen insight, delicate tact, and sound judgement, and he was generally admirable.

At a trial of any sort, needless to say, he was at his best. I can picture him now, rising to take his part with great deliberation. At first he would ask the witness or the defendant a few admirably chosen questions with the most nonchalant air. Then gradually he would warm to his work, and when it came to his speech, his eyes shone, his body swayed, and his arms worked with the excitement of debate, and the joy of conflict.

I was so very thankful when certain troubles which had kept Mawela away from his Communions, and away from his position of usefulness, were at last over, and he seemed definitely settled on the side of all that was best at the Mission.

Naturally all the Christians of the Nomlala clan, after Mengqupo's death, had looked to him as their father and adviser.

I quite hoped that he would have lived on for many years, and would become more and more useful.

One day, just as I had returned from seeing a sick man, I received a message to say that Mawela was ill and wanted to see me. I had heard that he was poorly, but did not think there was anything at all serious in his condition, and even when I saw him, and he himself told me he was dying, I quite thought he would soon recover.

I arranged to celebrate for him the next morning,
but at sunset he died.

How strange and incomprehensible it seems to our
limited vision that within a few months, Mawela and his
two Christian nephews, Wellington and Robert, should
all be taken away, while Nqwashu, Nqandeka, and
Qikani should all be left!

CHAPTER V

AUGUSTINE MTYATA

I AM interested to read what Mr. Kidd, in his book *The Essential Kafir*, says about the mental equipment of the Kafirs, as it quite confirms the results of my own experience.

In one place he says, 'Kafir boys are very quick in absorbing new ideas, and not infrequently make more rapid progress for a time than European boys . . . but at puberty there generally comes a gradual falling off of capacity, and the white boys then easily out-distance the black.'

How this is to be accounted for I really cannot say, but, although it seems to be a matter of general experience, there are many exceptions to the rule.

I used to feel that Alfred Mfono might have been one of the exceptions, if only he had had more stability of character.

He had an attractive face and excellent ability, but he was not very satisfactory. After leaving our school at Gqaqala, he went down to S. John's College, Umtata, and took his teacher's certificate. Unfortunately he did not prove a trustworthy teacher, and when he lost his place he went off to Johannesburg. We did not hear very satisfactory accounts of him from the gold mines, but after I had left the Mission he came back to S. Cuthbert's and begged Father Gerald to be allowed another trial as a teacher.

Father Gerald evidently did not encourage him much, and told him to look for some other employment first, so that he might prove the sincerity of his words.

Alfred went back to his home, and the following day sent this letter to Father Gerald :—

St. Patrick's, Gqaqala,
25. I. 04.

'DEAR FATHER,

'Having reached my house after we had spoken into a very deep contemplation on Kafir beer forsaking which represented well to me as being the most difficult problem that had ever occupied my intellect. So much did it prevail on my memory that I had not been able to sleep at all that night, and I concluded as you will hear later on.

'Although you have said I had better go to the office or be a policeman, &c., it seems to me that you are not at all pleased that I should do so; it is only because you cannot help it, and have not the means of changing me from what I am to what I am wanted to be. On my part I had been glad to go to the office just as I have been to teach, but all the time did not want to go to any kind of employment leaving you unsatisfied, and also for the following facts which dwell in my head. If a teacher say from mishap or misbehaviour of a pupil "You will fail", it will not be long before you see that. If a parent warn his child against anything, and the child goes on to do it again in spite of what his father have said, the results are often disastrous; hence I shall not go to any other place till this infamy and blot of untrustworthiness about me has been repaired, and what I have lost regained.

'This is how I have thought of dealing with it—firstly,

by giving up my great friend and taking a temperance medal ; secondly, by taking a school in your own parish.

'Though Kafir beer has been my first-rate beverage I have some confidence that by God's help I shall conquer it.

'I remember I had many companions who used to be just as I am, and some even worse, but now I am the only one of the company who is still left to indulge in it. The others have given it up but did not die, evidently I shall not, being made of the same material.

'Mfundisi, I want you to give me a school in your own parish so that I may have a trial, and see whether it is a magic that some of my schoolfellows have taken schools with me and have kept them ever since.

'I am, dear Father,
'Your obedient servant,
'ALFRED MFONO.'

That letter, written by a Kafir boy in English, certainly shows not only very peculiar Kafir characteristics of mental reasoning, but also considerable ability. I have quoted it and spoken of it because it forms an excellent introduction to my account of Augustine Mtyata, who was one of the 'schoolfellows who took schools' with Alfred, and 'have kept them ever since', and was also one of those who, although not indulging in excess, gave up Kafir beer and 'did not die'.

Augustine was the name of his baptism, and when I first knew him his name was Balekwa. I remember so well the day he first came to me, about twelve years ago.

I ought perhaps to mention here that S. Cuthbert's Mission is in the middle of the Pondomisi tribe, and that at that time the Christians of the tribe were very few, while the great majority of the people were not only heathen, but seemingly unresponsive and indifferent to missionary work.

Outside the limits of the Pondomisi tribe we had many centres of work, and large numbers of Christian people; so that the Pondomisi could hardly remain unaffected by Christianity, even although they might not respond to missionary effort.

We did not by any means give up preaching to the Pondomisi, but our main hope lay in training some of the children who were given over to us by their parents.

It was wonderful to see how quickly most of these children settled down with us and seemed to be perfectly happy under entirely new conditions of life.

This was so much the case that one really quite forgot that some of these little fellows who went to school, dug in the garden, and played cricket, had never seen anything else than a heathen kraal, and had known no other occupation than that of herding the sheep or the cattle.

When the sun shone and food was plentiful, the life of those little herd boys must have been a very pleasant one. The different flocks would be driven together so that the task of herding them might not be too burdensome, and then the joys of the day would begin. The sheep-skins or little bits of red-ochred blanket which served for clothing would be laid aside, the favourite calves would be mounted, and most exciting would be the races which followed. Then, too, what fun those little hunting parties would be—a semi-circle of naked little boys, each with his bundle of sticks beating the veld for small birds!

Better still was the repast which followed over the dung fire on the veld, when the spoils would all be rigidly shared.

Sometimes the pleasure was rather more exciting and a trifle risky, when one bull, well known for his fighting qualities, would—quite accidentally of course—be brought to feed on the same path as another bull of renown.

But it was not always so pleasant. Sometimes the crops failed, food was scarce, and then things did not look so bright. Often they would go out in the morning without tasting food, and would get nothing—not even at milking-time—until they returned at night.

Well, this was the sort of life that these youngsters had led, until one day they would find themselves marched off to the Mission station (very frequently by their own wish, and never against their will), sent down to the river to wash, clothed in a shirt, and beginning life under very different conditions.

We always tried to keep them Kafirs as far as possible, and to arrange that their mode of living should differ as little as possible from that of their homes. But even then, how strange it must all have seemed! The regular hours, the discipline, the attention to personal cleanliness, the school work, the industrial work, the games. . . . What could they think of them all at first?

Now that the confidence, not only of the boys but also of the heathen parents, has been more fully gained, the management of these 'boarders' has become much easier.

There is in the Kafir a certain amount of instinctive

AUGUSTINE.

To face page 57.

suspicion towards a stranger, but, when once his confidence has been won, he becomes very trustful.

When the children knew that they could run home, and that our discipline there would be disregarded, their management was not easy, but in most cases now, the parents themselves would bring the runaway back with perfect confidence that his punishment would be just.

All of them, young and old, have a great sense of justice, and when once they are persuaded that a thing is according to law and custom, they are quite satisfied.

Well! one day a young Pondomisi boy came to my hut and asked to talk with me. This boy was Balekwa, and he told me that his parents were dead, and that he was living with an Uncle and Aunt, but that he wanted to come to live with us and to be my son.

I have no doubt I took some steps to find out that the boy was speaking the truth, and that the Uncle agreed.

Balekwa was then a nice, bright-looking boy of eleven or twelve, and he very soon settled down to his new life as if he had never known any other.

It was always a pleasure to see how cheerful these boys were under nearly all circumstances.

I remember meeting an English lady who had travelled in Natal, and who told me that she thought the chief characteristic of the natives was a settled gloom. I was astonished to hear her say so, as I have always thought cheerfulness to be their most striking characteristic. I dare say the lady had only seen them in towns as servants, and one knows quite well that they can appear most unfavourably under conditions where they are not happy, or not understood.

Balekwa quite soon began to draw others to the Mission, and persuaded a sister of his—older than himself—to put herself under the care of our lady-workers. The sister soon tired of it and left, but Balekwa not only stayed on but expressed his desire to become a Christian.

We never pressed the boys at all in the matter of religion, as we wished any movement in that direction to be entirely spontaneous on their part. Of course they saw what religion meant—they saw people day by day practising it in various ways, and they heard of religion in school and in their morning and evening prayers, and on the days when all were expected to go to church.

I often wondered how much one of those new arrivals thought, and what he thought.

When Balekwa came to tell me that he wanted to become a Christian, he had no doubt previously talked the matter over with others of the boys who were already Christians.

The first step was to become a Catechumen, and probably on one of the following Sundays, he knelt with a few others outside the church door and was then admitted to the Catechumenate.

A year was the minimum length of the probation and instruction of a Catechumen, but Balekwa showed such earnestness of purpose and readiness of mind, that it certainly was no longer than a year in his case, and he was baptized with the name Augustine.

We had not then got an immersion font at the Mission, but in the new church this omission will be remedied.

However, the Service of Holy Baptism was always very impressive in our little church, each person receiv-

ing immediately after baptism a lighted taper, to remind
him (or her) of the obligations to the world around.
Soon after this Augustine was confirmed and became
a communicant.

While still at school, he and one or two others were
licensed to preach to the heathen, and, when he finally
passed out of our school, he was established as preacher
and teacher in one of the new centres among the
heathen. For a long time he had been looking forward
to marriage, and now his hopes were realized, and he
was married to a nice Christian girl who had been at
school with him.

Soon after their first boy was born, a friend of ours—
a missionary—came down from Mashonaland to pay us
a visit, and he was very anxious to find at least one
young man amongst our Christians who would go back
with him to begin work amongst the Matabele.

We called together our workers (preachers, teachers,
&c.), and our friend from Mashonaland told them all
about that country and of the heathen tribes.

A few days afterwards Augustine came to me, and
offered to go to work with my friend in the far-off
country.

On a certain day not long after this, three incidents
took place which I shall not easily forget.

1. A large congregation was assembled in our church,
and the Holy Eucharist was being celebrated. After
the Creed, Augustine came forward, and, kneeling at the
Altar-rails, was given a Bible and a crucifix. No words
could have spoken so eloquently of the work to which he
was called.

2. A little later a waggon with fourteen oxen came

slowly down the ridge opposite the Mission buildings, and inside the tent I caught my last glimpse of Augustine, his wife, and his son.

3. Later still in that same day I was stopping to see an English trader in his store, and while I was talking to him, a heathen girl in her red-ochred blanket came up to me and said 'How is Balekwa?' After a moment I recognized her as the sister who had come for a time to the Mission and had gone away. I had never seen her again until this very day, when her brother was leaving friends and home to go up to an unknown country at the call of God.

CHAPTER VI

MTSHAZI

THE first time I saw Mtshazi was at Whitby, in York-shire. My father had taken a house there for the summer, and he kindly allowed me to ask Mtshazi and his cousin, Daniel Mtangayi, to spend a week of their holidays with us.

It was with rather curious feelings that I went to the railway station to meet our guests. I had never seen a Kafir before, but I was hoping in a few months to join Canon Gibson (as he then was) at his Mission in Kaffraria. Mtshazi was the future chief of the Pondomisi, and it was amongst his people that I was destined to live for many years. For the present he and his cousin were being educated at Denstone College.

It was not difficult to recognize our guests among the passengers as the train drew up. Mtshazi was taller than Daniel by two or three inches, and was also rather lighter in colour. Although only about eighteen years of age, and a stranger in a foreign land, he already seemed to have an air of authority. Daniel was the elder of the two, and had a pleasant face and a rather hesitating manner. It was difficult to realize that they had only been in England about a year, and that five or six years previously they had been running about on the veld with a bit of red-ochred blanket for clothing.

There was no embarrassment in their greeting, and they displayed very little surprise at their surroundings.

Mtshazi's father, Mditshwa, had the distinction of being one of the two chiefs who headed the last native rebellion in South Africa—unless the Matabele could be said to have rebelled. He sided with Mhlonhlo after the murder of Mr. Hope, and when the outbreak was finally crushed, Mditshwa had been sent as a prisoner to Capetown. Eventually he was released, 'kissed the hand of the Government', and returned to settle among his people as a private individual without authority as a chief. It was at this time that he brought his son and four other boys to Canon Gibson at S. Cuthbert's Mission. 'They are not my sons any longer,' he said, 'they are your sons now. Take them and do whatever you like with them. Teach them all you know yourself. If they are troublesome, beat them. They are your sons now.'

In *Eight Years in Kaffraria*, we are told that these boys 'brought with them the whole of their personal property, consisting of one blanket apiece, which served for clothing in the day and bedclothes at night, and one pipe which was shared among the five . . .'. Mditshwa also sent a cow with them to be milked daily for their use, so that they might have 'amasi', the thick sour milk so much used by all natives.

Many a vision of hope must have centred round Mtshazi. Twenty years previously Bishop Key had begun work among the Pondomisi, but his reward had not come quickly. He had 'toiled all the night', and it must often have seemed that he had 'caught nothing'. When now the future chief was given over into the hands of the missionary, the prospect must have appeared to be very different.

I must pass over those early years in which Mtshazi was being trained, first at S. Cuthbert's and later at Lovedale. In 1890 Canon Gibson decided to send him to England, and called the chiefs of the tribe together to announce his intention. There was very little opposition on their part, and they only stipulated that he should not be kept too long ' across the sea '.

The dangers of an English education for a Kafir boy were fully realized, but both Canon Gibson himself and all those whom he consulted (including Bishop Key and the Chief Magistrate of Griqualand East), felt that the experiment ought to be made, even at the risk of disappointment and possible failure.

When he came to us at Whitby, Mtshazi had not yet been baptized, although he had expressed a desire in that direction. It was felt that ' his actual baptism in England would be an error, as the people might fairly complain of what would seem suspiciously like underhand dealing'. It was hoped that on his return to his own country he would be ready to face tribal opposition for the sake of his religion, and be publicly baptized in the face of his people.

Seeing Mtshazi in an English house, sharing our interests, entering with zest into English amusements, attending the services in the church, it seemed impossible to me to think of him as at all open to the suggestions of heathen life. At that time my ideas of heathen life were very vague, and I probably failed to dissociate it from barbarism. In England we see Kafir life very far off through the eyes of generally unsympathetic travellers. We see it in its weakness and inferiority. We cannot conceive of it as a possible rival to civilization and Christianity when once apprehended. We have a sort of vague consciousness that, in spite of all the defects and inconsistencies of social life in England, its superiority must be immediately manifest. We do not realize heathen life as distinct from savagery. We have no idea of the powers at work, nor of the cumulative force of tribal and family customs. We cannot understand that heathen public opinion may be as strong or even stronger than Christian public opinion.

As I look back upon those days Mtshazi spent with us at Whitby, I feel that I did not foresee the danger of his position, and his extraordinary need of strength of character. I seemed to think that the heathen life was necessarily left behind for ever, and that each day in England must widen the gulf between him and the past. To-day, with many years of experience behind me, I see that the choice does not necessarily lie between heathenism and a Christian civilization. The greatest danger of all is in civilized heathenism, where the man remains a heathen but adopts as much or as little of European custom as suits his fancy. Poor Mtshazi! as I walked and talked with him in those days at Whitby, I little realized what a struggle was before him. There was a good deal of reserve about him which I used to put down partly to unfamiliarity with English, but Daniel used to chat away very freely, and I learned a good deal from him about the land of my adoption.

When the week had elapsed, Mtshazi and his cousin went on to stay with other friends, and I saw them no more in England.

We met again under very different circumstances less than a year later. A day had been fixed for a meeting

PONDOMISI MEETING AT S. CUTHBERT'S.

To face page 65.

of the Pondomisi at S. Cuthbert's Mission. The son of
Mditshwa was then to be given back to his tribe. Long
had they waited for this day to arrive.

Loyalty to the chief is the first and great command
of Kafir life, and Mditshwa's action in giving his son to
the missionary had met with outward respect. But the
strain upon obedience had doubtless been very great.
Custom governs the Kafir mind, and the Pondomisi
must often have trembled for the continuance of old traditions during the years in which Mtshazi was receiving
education. But if the meeting was awaited with anxiety
by the Pondomisi, there were others who had even
greater cause for anxiety. One thought of some of those
meetings in the early dawn of English history when
Christianity was solemnly weighed against the prevalent
heathenism. In the present instance so much seemed
to depend upon the decision of character of the young
chief, and this was, as yet, rather an unknown quantity.

In no way is the common idea of Kafirs as savages so
completely contradicted as in a public meeting. I often
think some of our Members of Parliament might pro-
fitably learn some lessons of behaviour from these
so-called 'savages' in their meetings. The chief has
far less trouble in maintaining order than the Speaker in
the House of Commons.

At a big meeting of this sort speakers are always chosen
beforehand, and the proceedings are very orderly. When
all had assembled, Canon Gibson began by explaining
the object of the meeting. Mditshwa's request had been
complied with, and his son Mtshazi had been 'educated'
by the missionary. He had been across the sea to Eng-

land, and had seen the country of the great Queen. Now he was given back to the people.

Then followed many speeches from the chosen representatives, all taking the line of resistance to any change in the old customs. I can picture one of these speakers in particular. This was old Ranuka, one of Mtshazi's uncles. He has a remarkably clear way of speaking, and combines very deliberate enunciation with a large share of the musical cadence which is so characteristic of the speech of the people. Always polite and courteous, Ranuka began by expressing the pleasure of the tribe at seeing Mtshazi among them once more, and their gratitude to Canon Gibson for all he had done. Then he turned to the main point. They wanted their chief to walk in the well-trodden paths. In particular he maintained that a chief must not be bound to only one wife, and that his position could only be kept up by the usual freedom in this respect. Even Mtshazi's mother was present and actually spoke, supporting the words of other speakers with great vehemence. One could see that in her, Christianity had a formidable antagonist.

At last Mtshazi himself rose to speak, and great was the silence with which his quietly-spoken words were received. It seemed so strange to see him standing there in that position, when so short a time previously I had seen him sitting in an English drawing-room.

He told the people that he had seen Christianity and civilization for himself, and that his mind was now made up. He had decided to become a Christian, and to support the work of the missionaries among his people.

So ended this long-looked-for meeting. The people

returned to their homes, and we felt that a new day had dawned among the Pondomisi. All promised so well. Mtshazi was baptized, taking the name of Edwardes. He was also recognized by the Government as chief, and in this recognition the people saw pardon for their share in the late rebellion.

Mtshazi now began to build for himself the 'ikomkulu' (great place) of a chief. When Mditshwa, his father, was released from prison, he established himself upon the shoulder of a hill which must have been the scene of many a fight between his people and their aggressive neighbours the Pondos.

At his death, according to the usual custom in the case of a chief, his huts were vacated, and the place where he lived and was buried, was marked only by a heap of poles taken from his cattle kraal. Within a hundred yards of that grave, Mtshazi now built his new home.

The kraal is like all others, except that the huts seem to be rather larger and more numerous. One of the huts is different from the rest, and is the only outward mark that 'times have changed'. This hut shows some advance of ideas: it is smaller than the others, but has properly made doors and window, and an upright, well-thatched roof. Inside this hut further marks of progress are seen in the simple furniture, the pictures on the walls, and a few books, including a Bible, on the shelf.

Such was the home the young chief made for himself, and our hope was that he would soon marry a Christian wife, and would become a strong leader of his people. Before very long, there were indications that our hopes were not to be realized. First one thing was whispered, and then another, until faces became grave, and the future began to look very overcast.

It was at this time that Canon Gibson felt it right to accept an offer made him by the Bishop of Capetown, to join him as his coadjutor Bishop. Before his departure from S. Cuthbert's, a meeting of the Pondomisi was called for a last farewell to him, and to give me to the people as his successor. This meeting gave an opportunity of seriously warning Mtshazi, and the Pondomisi in his presence, of the dangers of a downward path. Very strong words were spoken, but the people seemed to 'care little for these things', and Mtshazi's attitude was evasive and unsatisfactory.

Humanly speaking, it was very unfortunate that at such a critical time there should have been a change of pilot. The Kafirs, it is true, have a great sense of the authority which resides in office. They would recognize me as 'u-Key' in the same way that they had recognized Bishop Gibson before me. But, at such a moment of contending currents, one feels that the withdrawal of the personal influence of my predecessor was especially to be deplored. Fortunately Bishop Key was still with us, although the many demands of the Diocese allowed him but few opportunities of visiting the Pondomisi.

Many people are inclined to think that the rapid lapse of the young chief was due to complete insincerity. It has been thought that he was never at heart a Christian, but that he wanted to sit on both sides of the fence. He wanted, it has been said, to conciliate the missionaries and the Government on the one hand, while, on the other, he followed all the traditions of heathen life, and thus retained popularity among the majority of the people. It is, of course, quite impossible to decide the question positively, but I do not think these conclusions are quite warranted by the facts.

On the whole, I think it more likely that he meant what he said at the first meeting, and that the subsequent pressure of tribal influence, added to the persuasions of a masterful mother, were too powerful for him. I do not think he has ever shown himself to be a strong character, and it is quite possible that, secretly, his sense of the obligations of his baptism was a very insufficient one. Perhaps he also claimed for himself a very indulgent view of the requirements of Christianity in consequence of his position as chief. Such an attitude would leave him singularly open to the attacks of a militant heathenism.

There is, no doubt, one consideration which might have disarmed the attack of the heathen element, and have strengthened Mtshazi's resistance. If the Government had regarded faithfulness to Christianity as a condition of its favour, there might have been an outward compliance.

I *do not* think this would have been either possible or satisfactory, but it must be remembered that the apparent dissociation between Government and Christianity must have been very puzzling to the Pondomisi mind. They would be apt to attribute to indifference a delicate reserve on the part of the Government in regard to Christianity. Hitherto they had had little opportunity of seeing that the sphere of magistrate and missionary were not identical. Their first missionary, 'u-Key' must have seemed to them closely associated with the Government.

He had often been the mediator between themselves and the Government, and possibly they had an exaggerated sense of his connexion with it. They had seen the same thing with his successor, 'u-Gibson'. It was to him that Mditshwa had turned after his release, and it was he who had pleaded his cause before the Government. It now seemed that loss of favour with the missionary did not involve loss of favour with the Government. It is true that the Chief Magistrate spoke strong words of warning to Mtshazi and to the people, but it was quite clear nevertheless that, although Mtshazi might turn aside from the ways of the missionary, he would still be recognized as chief by the Government. Many of them would be genuinely sorry that there should be a breach between their chief and their missionary. But, after all, the favour of the Government was a much more substantial and tangible thing than that of the missionary, and no doubt they quite expected that in course of time the latter would be reconciled, and a happy compromise effected. The more I think of it, the more I come to realize the enormous difficulties of Mtshazi's position. Nothing but the most loyal surrender to grace could have saved him.

In addition to more obvious difficulties, it was inevitable that he should feel keenly the difference of treatment on the part of the white people in his own country from that of his friends in England. That is the supreme danger of an English education for a native. I do not now go into the question of which is the better and wiser treatment, but it cannot be doubted that the constant sense of this difference must have been very injurious at such a critical moment.

In course of time Mtshazi had taken to himself many wives, and there could no longer be any doubt as to his position. We now had to face the serious question of our attitude to him. His position was, unfortunately, not altogether unique. There were other instances of chiefs who had been baptized and had succumbed to the heathen influences around them. These men now adopted a sort of half and half attitude which was particularly confusing to the minds of their people. On the one hand, they lived as heathen, followed heathen customs, married many wives; but, on the other hand, they posed as patrons of education and Christianity. They established schools, patronized church-openings, and gave gifts to Church work. This was undoubtedly the sort of position which Mtshazi would have adopted, and, *from one point of view*, the interests of the Mission would have been greatly advanced by allowing him to do so. It seemed to us, however, that although outward progress would have been greater, the whole tone of Christianity would have been lowered by our consent to such an arrangement. The Church in those parts was yet in its infancy, and discipline was with us a real thing. Binding, as well as loosing, was a recognized part of our Lord's commission. Surely both for the individual and for the Christians at large, it was better to write in capital letters the Church's hostility to sin, and her refusal to make compromises with it. We felt that any appearance of profiting by Mtshazi's influence as chief, would be regarded as a condoning of his sin. This would be fatal both for him and the people.

Eventually, after due warning and much pleading, the Bishop's letter of excommunication was publicly read in all the churches of our parish, and Mtshazi's position was made absolutely clear.

Years have passed, and there is little sign that Mtshazi is coming to himself. At various times I have had interviews with him, but it has always seemed to me that what he would like is merely an outward reconciliation in the relationship between himself and the missionaries. Our Christian people often tell me 'Mtshazi has a conscience, and will one day return.' His cousin, Daniel Mtangayi, who remains a faithful Christian, and has built a home which he calls 'Grosvenor House' (!), is also hopeful at times.

There are now many Christians among the Pondomisi, and one has the satisfaction of knowing that in their case there has been no blind following of a Christian chief. It is not altogether visionary to hope that the very people who once cried out that they wanted a chief who would walk in the trodden paths of heathen life, will some day urge his return to *the* path which he promised to follow on the day of his baptism.

OUT STATION CHURCH—EXTERIOR.

To face page 73.

CHAPTER VII

JIMUEL

SOME time ago I received a letter from my friend Jimuel, of which I give this translation :—

'DEAR MFUNDISI,

'I thank you for your letter and for your kindness in writing to me. . . .

'I must now tell you our news. On August 24, I went to S. Cuthbert's for the Confirmation, to which numbers of people went from the out-stations. I went with fifteen people from this place who had all been accepted for Confirmation. . . .

'On the same day I, with Alban Maka and two others, went up before the Altar to receive from the Bishop my licence as a catechist.

'It was there that I began when I was quite young to work for God.

'Just as S. Paul calls Timothy his son in the Faith, so am I your son.

'I remember to-day those early days at S. Cuthbert's, when I used to cook in the kitchen, and dig in the garden.

'But in all that work I was being trained for the work of preaching the "message of peace" to our people.

'Do not forget me, Mfundisi, in your prayers. Pray for me that I do not lose myself and that I do not get weak and tired in this work of God. Help me, too, by giving thanks for this work which is given to me.

'I hope to go to S. Bede's Theological College in February, so that I may receive more training there. . . .

'With sincere "salutations", not only from myself but from all your children here.

'I am, your son,
'JIMUEL.'

Now please do not say that the writer must be a 'prig' or 'insincere'—because he uses language which would not be equally natural to you. Remember that he was not born in England, where there is an exceedingly great diffidence about using any religious language outside the pulpit.

If he had been born in England with a white skin, I will try to tell you exactly the sort of person he would have been.

In the first place he would have been called James, not Jimuel, and his friends would have begun by calling him 'Jim', and then 'dear old Jim'.

At school he would have been one of those conscientious, plodding fellows who work themselves up nearly to the top of each form in turn. He would have been considered by no means brilliant, but not thick-skulled. He would have been chaffed a good deal for sticking to his books, but he would have been nearly always good-humoured over it, and would have said, 'Oh! I am not like you clever fellows who can get on without sweating.'

The results of his toil would always have been at the disposal of the more indolent. He would not have been good at games, but might have turned out a fair 'full-back' at football.

His own general conduct would always have been good,

but he would not have taken a very active part in protesting against what was bad on the part of others.

Just occasionally he might have worked himself up to making some very good-natured protest. At the same time, evil would have slunk away naturally from him, and, very reluctantly on his part, he would have been pushed up into positions of responsibility.

Then he would have gone up to the 'Varsity', and would have gradually become stronger in character, but without much personal ambition.

He would have been generally liked, but the clever people would have called him rather dull and obtuse. Wilder spirits would have thought him a bit of an old woman, but they would have had a certain respect for him.

At the 'Varsity' he would have taken no very decided steps in influencing his generation from a religious point of view, but he would probably have taken a class in a Sunday-school.

Then he would have gone on to a Theological College, and through much distrust of self his character would have been greatly deepened. He would always have a wholly undue sense of the superiority of intellectual people, and would groan over the idea of his future sermons and other responsibilities.

Then would have come the first curacy, and to his own surprise, he would have found that he was gaining day by day a remarkable influence over the men and boys of the parish. . . .

Well! he was born, not in England, but in Africa, with a black skin, not a white, and he was called Jimuel, not James. His parents both owed their conversion to Pres-

byterians, but it happened that his father became a
' squatter ' on a white man's farm, not very far from one
of our out-stations, and Jimuel was sent to one of our
schools.

In the ordinary course of events he, no doubt, would
have been removed from school at the age of fourteen,
and would have gone home to live with his father and
become a sort of farm labourer. However, things were
ordered differently. It happened that we wanted at
S. Cuthbert's a useful boy who could be taught to do
our cooking and could employ his spare time in the
garden.

On my next visit to Gqaqala I inquired of the teacher
if he knew of a boy whom he could recommend, and he
promptly named Jimuel.

The father's consent was obtained, and instead of going
to plough the lands and milk the cows, he came down to
S. Cuthbert's to spend his time in cooking.

The kitchen was exceedingly dismal and dark, but
this did not seem to distress Jimuel, who before long
became a very treasured inmate of our establishment.

He did not give up his books, and used to attend
a night-school.

In course of time I saw quite clearly that it would be
wicked to keep him in the kitchen, and he was sent to
our school with the condition that in his spare time he
was still to work for us.

I must confess the sacrifice was not an easy one. It
was indeed nice to think that some day we might have an
excellent teacher or preacher, but a reliable and good
servant was such a treasure that the temptation was
great to keep him.

He was confirmed while still at S. Cuthbert's, and he used to go out on Sundays with a preacher, amongst the heathen.

Then the day came when Jimuel had reached the top 'rung' of the educational ladder provided at the Mission school.

Once a year the inspector, appointed by Government, comes round to examine our schools. Sad it is when the inspector impresses us all with the idea that the only object of education is to pass an examination. Fortunately some of our inspectors take not only a real interest in the natives, but are heartily opposed to such a narrow view of education.

It is very seldom that we know the exact date of the inspector's visit; in fact sometimes there is an evident desire to take us by surprise. Naturally the excitement is very great amongst the children when the first news arrives that he is in the district.

Immediately, the attendance improves, and sleepy heads begin to wake up. Suddenly one morning a 'buggy' is seen on the opposite hill. Up it comes to the Mission buildings. There is a moment of great distraction, as all eyes are turned upon a strange gentleman who descends from his buggy and walks towards the school.

The teacher shouts 'stand', and then the half dreaded, half hoped-for, visitor walks in, and the examination begins.

In the top standard (vi), while we are proud of the success of the children, we cannot help being sorry when they pass. It means such a change. For years they have come day by day to that school; they have come

under the influence of teachers and clergy; they have
contributed their little share to the life of the whole;
sometimes their share has been bad, sometimes good,
but bad or good, when the day comes that the inspector
marks 'pass' against their names, one cannot help being
sorry. If they are good we want them still—we want
their influence and their help. If they are bad, we want
them too. So much of the badness is our own fault—
the fault of our own neglect or carelessness. We want to
try again, and we want them to try again. We are
afraid of their plunge into the outside world. Perhaps
they will go to the gold mines, perhaps to Capetown;
and how will they fare there?

It was quite a blow when Jimuel got his 'pass', and
it was decided that he should for the present go on to
S. John's College, which is chiefly an institution for the
training of native teachers.

We are generally a little bit afraid of meeting one of
our boys after he has spent six months at that College.
The Warden is admirable and the teaching good; but it
so often happens that higher education seems to go along
with higher collars, higher heels, and other accessories,
which seem to denote a certain loss of manliness and a
disinclination for honest toil.

Perhaps though, now we are missionaries, some of us
are inclined to forget the colour of our waistcoats, and
the size of our 'checks', and a few other vanities belonging to the days of youth.

Jimuel, however, did not disappoint our expectations
of his character at S. John's College, and in course of
time he became a teacher at one of our out-stations.

We talk of the temptations of our cities and towns, and

OUT STATION CHURCH—INTERIOR.

To face page 79.

undoubtedly they are very great, but I doubt if any one
has quite such a fire to go through as a young unmarried
native teacher living alone at an out-station, where there
are a few Christians, many heathen, and some who have
set themselves free from the social customs and restraints
of heathen life, without accepting the obligations of
Christianity.

When a young man comes out of that fire unscathed,
I always think of Shadrach, Meshach, and Abed-nego,
and I always know that there was some One else walking
with him in the fire of that temptation, and His Form
was like ' the Son of God '.

So when a man comes out of the fire without ' a hair of
his head singed . . . nor the smell of fire upon him ' he
must surely be a strong man, and that is what I felt
about our friend, when he left his first school, and went
to S. Bede's Theological College to be trained as a
catechist.

His letter tells us that the results of that training were
satisfactory, and that he now has the Bishop's licence.

At the present moment I believe he is working tem-
porarily at Ncembu, until he can once more return to
the Theological College for further training, with a view
to the diaconate.

I am glad to think of him at Ncembu, because the
work there has always interested me so much.

I remember when I first went out, I was asked by
Bishop Gibson to go up to Ncembu, and see if the chief
Bikwe would not allow us to begin work amongst his
people. That was my first experience of a large meeting
of heathen men, and it impressed me a good deal.

The chief Bikwe, with his sharp intelligent face, and

abrupt incisive manner, sat out under his cattle kraal, with all his men in their ochred blankets sitting or lying about him. I, with my interpreter, sat near Bikwe, and explained the object of the meeting. Then Bikwe invited the men to speak, and several of them had their say. All of them are accustomed to plead their own cases before the chief, and are lawyers, or at least advocates, through that experience. Some of them, too, are real orators, and have a very persuasive way of speaking.

It makes me sad sometimes to see notebooks and pencils and other European 'aids', used by our Christian natives, as I fear the inevitable destruction of those wonderful memories and gifts of eloquence which distinguish so many of them.

After a certain amount of talking, permission was asked by Bikwe's men to withdraw for a freer discussion amongst themselves. After a time they returned, and Bikwe's chief councillor, speaking in the name of the chief, announced the decision.

They were, he said, not yet ready for these things, but some day they would be ready, and then they would turn to S. Cuthbert's Mission.

That was not an idle promise. Some years afterwards a message arrived from Bikwe to the effect that he and his people would now like us to send a preacher and a teacher. Gladly we complied with their request; a humble start was made, and now the work has grown to one of great importance.

I feel quite sure that Jimuel will not be building hay and stubble upon the foundation which has been laid there. I do not think he will 'set the Thames on fire'. He will not be the leader of any great movement, nor will his be

the influential voice which will move the assemblies of
learned men.

But some day will come times of storm and stress, and
then, when some are being driven in one direction and
some in another, the Church in those parts will possess in
Jimuel a very rock of strength and steadfastness.

. . . .

While the 'proof' of the above is in my hand, a letter
has come from one of the Clergy at S. Cuthbert's, in
which he says, 'Jimuel has gone to S. Bede's College,
Umtata. I am always thanking God for the work he
(Jimuel) has done at Ncembu. Although he was only
there eight months, the people are full of sorrow that he
has left them.'

CHAPTER VIII

KANYELWA

IT was a very busy time, but a message from Kanyelwa was not to be disregarded. Again and again I read over those few lines of Xosa (Kafir language) scribbled on the back of an old envelope. The messenger who had brought the note stood before me, a tall heathen lad with his red-ochred blanket thrown loosely round him. He had evidently hurried considerably over those ten miles, as the beads of perspiration still stood on his forehead. In vain I questioned him for more particulars than could be gleaned from the envelope. 'Andazi' (I don't know), was the one answer. For the last time I read over the scrawl. 'Mfundisi, I want to see you. If you will make haste you will find me at Xokonxa. I am Kanyelwa.' I hesitated no longer, but called a native boy and told him to bring in a horse as soon as possible.

In the meantime I wondered why Kanyelwa was at Xokonxa, so far from his home; and why he should send over such an urgent message for me.

In those days, when the pressure of work was great, we were obliged to make strict rules about sending for the priest. So often I had been sent for from a great distance, had given up some engagements, and found on arrival that the sick person who was the object of the visit had recovered.

But Kanyelwa was not the man to send an idle message. He was a fine old man and a devout Christian. In former days he had been a preacher, and had served the Church very faithfully ; but, before my arrival at the Mission, he had been obliged to give up responsible work. He had been visited with some strange sickness which affected his hands and his feet. He himself used to tell me that it originated in a wetting while crossing a river, when the waters had come down very suddenly. I thought otherwise, but held my peace.

In course of time I had very little doubt that poor Kanyelwa was a leper. The Government rules were strict about leprosy, and, in addition to Robben Island, a new ' Segregation Camp' had been formed for native lepers at Emjanyana, which was about seventy miles distant from us. In the case of Kanyelwa, conscience did not persuade me that it was necessary to be an ' informer '. Clearly his leprosy was not tuberculous, and it seemed to be arrested. Besides, he was an old man, and his children were all grown up. Scientists now hold, I believe, that, at any rate in non-tuberculous leprosy, there is not nearly the same danger to others as in phthisis.

The very thought of separating poor old Kanyelwa from his home and family made me shudder. How easy it is to pass laws and to approve of them in the abstract ! I began to realize what our poor people in England think about the ' house '.

Kanyelwa must have been finely built when younger ; even when I knew him he was a tall, upright, dignified man, and there was a strange pathos in looking from the well set-up shoulders, and the bright intelligent face, to the poor hands and feet.

He lived at Esiqunqwini, the place where he had

worked as a preacher. He had become a convert as a grown-up man, when he had two wives and two families. One of the wives—also a convert—was, after their baptism, married to him with Christian rites; and a home was made close by for the other wife and her family. Kanyelwa had built a tiny hut in his own kraal, in which the missionary could stay on the occasion of his monthly visit to Esiqunqwini. This hut became my 'prophet's chamber' when I succeeded Bishop Gibson at S. Cuthbert's, and it possessed correctly the 'table, the stool, and the candlestick'.

How well I remember the visits to Esiqunqwini and the nights spent in that little hut! Kanyelwa's kraal, like most Kafir kraals, was built on a ridge coming down from the mountain, and from there we looked down into the valley of the Tsitsa river, with the ploughing lands of mealies and Kafir corn on either side. Almost immediately below was the little sod-walled, thatch-roofed church, which the Christians had built for themselves. Our custom was to arrive at an out-station of this sort in the afternoon. At Esiqunqwini old Kanyelwa would generally be waiting to greet me, and would call to a boy to off-saddle my horse. Then I would walk down to the church and ring the bell, unless the preacher had already done so. In some of these places the 'bell' was a very primitive arrangement, consisting sometimes of the tire of a waggon wheel tied up outside the church and a piece of plough-share with which it was beaten; but at Esiqunqwini we had a fine deep-toned bell, which could be heard for some miles. Far as its sound would carry, it could not reach all our people, many of whom came from distances of seven and eight miles.

Small Christian Children.

To face page 85.

Then one had a few minutes to prepare for the service and to collect one's thoughts for the sermon.

Gradually the people would arrive by twos and threes until it became time for the second bell. Evensong would be sung very heartily, and then, after the sermon, all intending communicants would remain for the preparation office.

After this some of the people might wish to see the priest for confession, and it would generally be nearly dark when I mounted once more to the little hut at Kanyelwa's kraal. As I passed the 'kitchen' hut of the kraal I could see that preparations were going on for an evening meal. Through the dense smoke which was coming out of the doorway could be seen figures bending over black cooking-pots, and, when I reached my own hut, I found the table covered with a white cloth and other signs which told a similar tale. Sometimes, I must confess, these signs were a little premature, but at length Kanyelwa's daughters would appear bearing the food, consisting generally of tea, bread, and some nice beans. After supper I sometimes went in to have a talk with Kanyelwa, who would be sitting over a wood fire in his large hut. We generally talked about the affairs of the Church in that place, in which he always took the keenest interest. Next morning, at sunrise, the bell would again send its deep tones travelling up the various valleys around, and soon we would once more be assembled in church for the monthly Eucharist. Some of the people there met together were isolated converts at a heathen kraal; others belonged to families entirely Christian. Latterly poor old Kanyelwa had not been able to be present in church, so after the service I used to take the

Blessed Sacrament to him in his hut. Very reverently did the old man make his Communion, and I still see that bright expectant look in his eyes. I do not think it would have been a great surprise to him if the earthly veil had then fallen aside.

.   .   .   .

Once more I reflected—what could this hasty summons to Xokonxa mean? Could it be that the old man was being called for the long journey? Or could it be that the Government . . . No! this last thought was intolerable. I thought again of Kanyelwa and his home—the patriarch cared for by loving hands. And then I thought of a visit I had paid to the Native Leper Asylum at Emjanyana. It was a very hot day of summer when I arrived at the top of the hill looking down into the Emjanyana valley. There, at some distance from one another, were two large groups of buildings roofed with corrugated iron, upon which the African sun beat fiercely down. In one of these were the women, and in the other the men.

Yes, they were admirably treated; they were tended and cared for by willing and skilful hands, ruled over by a magistrate who was a humane and good gentleman. As I got off my horse and stood looking down upon those buildings, and as, a little later, I went on a tour of inspection, I thought it an admirable institution. I do not remember thinking very much of the awful uprooting that had taken place when each one of those four hundred lepers had been caught away from home and friends. But at that time I did not personally know a leper in his own home. Some ignorant people are prone to think that where there is plenty to eat and to drink there is the Kafir's home. I did not think that, but perhaps in those days I hardly knew all that 'home' meant for the Kafir.

To-day, with that dirty envelope in my hand, I thought of those corrugated iron buildings, and I thought of Kanyelwa's home. Was this the meaning of his urgent message?

I got on my pony, and rode off to Xokonxa. When I arrived there any lingering hope I had was soon dispelled. 'Yes,' said a native policeman whom I questioned, 'the Government has found some lepers. There are the waggons, and they are going to Emjanyana.' 'Is Kanyelwa Mpazi from Esiqunqwini among them?' 'Yes, he is over there in those huts, waiting until the waggons are ready to start.'

As I walked over to the huts, I felt that two men were speaking within me. One man was saying, 'This is brutal and utterly unnecessary! All these years poor old Kanyelwa has been just the same. No one has been infected, although his children eat out of the same dishes. I will side with Kanyelwa, and cry out upon the Government.' Said the other man, 'This may not seem necessary to you, but the Government must be impartial. Besides, you are a priest, and what have you been teaching Kanyelwa all these years? Are you now going to tell him that all you have said about surrender to the will of God is untrue?' I walked on into one of the huts, and there I saw a company of sad-faced heathen people who, doubtless, were some of the relatives of other newly-found lepers. I could feel for these people to-day more than I should have been able to do if I had not known Kanyelwa. I wandered on, looking for my friend, and presently I found him lying in another hut all alone. At once he raised himself up, and the eager bright look came again into his eyes as he saw me coming in. Very soon the whole story was told—told as graphically as only a Kafir can tell a story. Suddenly, unexpectedly, the Government waggon had appeared at Esiqunqwini. Perhaps there was mercy in the suddenness, for all the minutes were wanted for action, and there was less time to think.

The two wives had been allowed to come so far with him, and they had now gone to buy something at the trader's store for his journey.

The author of *The Simple Life* has said in one of his books: 'In those hours when the *cry of blood* makes itself heard, to teach us by experience the strength of natural ties, a father is a father, a son a son, a mother a mother, little matter the customs, the laws, the times, or the social estate.' The 'cry of blood' certainly made itself heard now as I had not often heard it.

When Kanyelwa had finished the story he said, with tears in his bright eyes, 'Father, it seems that God has got some work for me to do at Emjanyana.'

Once more the positions were reversed. I was the pupil: he was the teacher.

. . . .

Some time afterwards I heard that Kanyelwa was doing a real evangelistic work at Emjanyana. I have not heard of him for some time, but I have little doubt that, as I always knew him, so should I find him now— a single-hearted faithful labourer in his Master's vineyard.

CHAPTER IX

J. M. AND J. M.

THERE are two men at the Mission who always go together in my mind, and I seem to find it quite impossible to write of one without the other.

As I sat down to write of them I decided not to use their full names but their initials only, and then to my surprise I realized that they have the same initials, so they shall be known as J. M. senior and J. M. junior.

To my mind, the real pleasure of missionary work begins when one can count real friends amongst the natives.

In the early days of one's 'apprenticeship' this pleasure is denied, and for some time the sense of aloofness is keenly felt. The primal difficulty is actually one of recognition, as at first the general likeness seems to obscure in one's mind the real distinctions of face and form. Even dress is not to be relied upon, as there is considerable freedom about borrowing garments. I remember being particularly anxious to distinguish between two brothers who were much alike. One of them was my servant, and I found myself constantly giving orders to the wrong boy. I decided to avoid confusion by giving *my* boy a very distinctive shirt, and on the following morning, delighting in the anticipated success of my plan, I hailed the boy with the shirt and told him to clean my saddle. A curious smile came over the boy's face, which prompted me to say: 'Well, you are Walter, are you not?' 'No, sir, I am Philip,' was the crushing reply.

Then, when one is no longer troubled by this difficulty of recognition, there remain the greater difficulties of language and manner of thought. Bishop Key used to say that he was often so absorbed in thinking of some unfamiliar word or construction used by the person to whom he was talking, that he completely lost the substance of his remarks. More often, I fear, the native loses the substance of our remarks because our words and construction are very unfamiliar to him. At last the happy day comes when friendly intercourse becomes possible, and then some of the best joys of missionary work begin.

It is always a real happiness to me to have the opportunity of visiting the people in their own kraals.

That most admirable Report of the South African Native Affairs Commission says: 'In their homes the natives are a hospitable and social people, clever and bright in repartee, fond of music, open-hearted and generous hosts, imitative and tractable, and interesting in many ways.'

This is a general description, but, of course, the people differ very much in different places. I should immensely like to be able to carry my readers with me to visit J. M. senior and J. M. junior in their own homes.

A Kafir hut is not always the most desirable place to inhabit for long. It is true that it is generally picturesque, but in some other respects there is much room for improvement. Christianity and civilization have been blamed rather frequently and vigorously for destroying the picturesque, and, it must be confessed, not without reason. Strange and incongruous it does seem to see emerging from the primitive hut of a heathen kraal, a native woman clothed, not in the red-ochred blanket of the people around her, but in a flimsy European dress, including high-heeled boots and a parasol. Worse still it is to be present at a Christian wedding on an occasion when the poor bridegroom is funereally dressed in the black clothes in which his English brother deems it proper to go to church, and the bride is arrayed in bridal costume, including the veil and artificial orange blossom.

The ordinary person is perpetually being 'put off' by these incidental and superficial results of civilization and missionary work. He very soon joins the ranks of those who do not even 'damn with faint praise' the efforts of missionaries.

But it is just here that the Report quoted above takes such a sane and large-minded line. Missionaries have said the same thing before, but they are not supposed to have an open mind about these things. Here is what the Report says: 'The great powers of Christianity and education are at work. There has been, and there continues, a great struggle between the powers of good and evil, of light and darkness, of enlightenment and ignorance, of progress and tradition, of Christianity and heathenism. Is it therefore surprising that much of what was picturesque, attractive, and admirable in the Native, when untouched by European influences, has been swept away? The final outcome of righteous war is not to be judged by the devastations of opposing armies, or by the scenes of bloodshed on the field of battle. No less fallacious would be the attempt to gauge the eventual issues of the civilization of the Natives by the many unfortunate features of the struggle which still prevail.'

Sad it is that the picturesque has to be lost; but there are occasions when, even in the realm of material advantage, the compensations have been very great.

I have heard many a visitor from England expatiate upon the picturesque aspect of the interior of a heathen Kafir hut, but I have only known one man who did not prefer a Christian's hut for a night's lodging, and he was generally said to have a 'bee in his bonnet'. Fortunately, in the exterior, at any rate, very little of the picturesque is lost by the improved construction of a Christian kraal.

At the kraal of both J. M. senior and J. M. junior you would see nothing at all out of harmony with Kafir characteristics, but you would see evidences of progress, industry, and skill. The huts themselves are large and well built, with properly made doors and windows, the roofs are lofty, and the thatching bears evidence of trained hands. Below the huts are gardens enclosed with sod walls, and carefully cultivated for fruit and vegetables. When you walk inside one of the huts, the difference from the heathen home is still more noticeable. There is no crouching down to avoid the extremely low limit of the doorway, no straining of eyes on account of darkness and pungent smoke, no flutter of disturbed fowls, no general sense of dirt and red ochre.

There are, I am sorry to say, a great many dirty and untidy huts in Christian kraals, but certainly it is with a real sense of pleasure that one looks in upon the huts of our friends, the J. M.'s; all is clean, simple, and orderly; the only objection I could make is to the mural decora-

J. M., JUNIOR.

To face page 93.

tions. Poor J. M. junior happens to be a very delicate man, who is constantly in the hands of doctors. Recently he has taken to 'Pink pills for pale people', and hearing that there was a reduction on a large order, he sent his 17s. 6d. to Capetown, and a supply of pink pills duly arrived, sufficient for an army. The proprietors of this famed medicine are not bashful in proclaiming its merits, and J. M. junior received many large wall-sheets with photos of prominent people, and expressions of their gratitude written in excellent Xosa. These wall-sheets I should like to see removed from the walls, but otherwise I see very little to criticize, and much to admire.

It is hardly surprising that I should connect the two J. M.'s together. They both happened to be leading men on the Mission, and I am thankful to say their lead is always a good one. They live near one another, are great friends, plough together, reap together, saw timber in the forest together, and to a large extent seem to think together.

This harmony is rather remarkable when one considers how widely different were the circumstances of their early lives.

J. M. senior belongs to the Swazi nation, and not only speaks Xosa with quite a foreign accent, but is himself quite different in looks from the Transkei Kafirs.

He has never told me much of his early life, but he seems to have travelled about the country a good deal in doing work of different sorts. At one time he was a waggon driver, at another a post-cart driver, at another a private servant. He became a Christian, and married a most excellent wife, long before he came to S. Cuthbert's.

J. M. junior, on the other hand, is a Fingo, and the

son of Christian parents. He was brought up under
missionary influences, received an education in Mission
schools, and nearly all the work of his early life was
as a teacher. He, too, is married to a good wife, and
has a family of young children.

Both men have now been at S. Cuthbert's Mission
a great many years, and have witnessed its growth from
early days.

J. M. senior is regarded as the leading man on the
Mission under the missionary, in matters connected
directly with its spiritual and moral welfare. J. M. junior
is the leading man in affairs secular. As a matter of
fact, the two provinces cannot clearly be distinguished,
and my chief object in writing this is to show how
valuable both men have been, and are, in the work of
the Mission.

I remember hearing some English traders talking
rather disparagingly one day of Christian natives. I
ventured to join in the conversation, and singled out
J. M. junior as a good representative of a Christian
Kafir. One of my trader friends immediately said, ' Oh,
yes, we can all trust J. M. If he came to my store
to-day and asked for all the contents, I would let him
have them, and should feel no uneasiness about the payment.' That is just the sort of man J. M. junior is—he
inspires confidence, and as he also possesses a remarkably
good head, he is invaluable as the director of all the
practical affairs of the Mission. I cannot say what a
comfort it has been to me to be able to rely upon such
a man.

There are endless questions continually cropping up
connected with the plough lands, the cattle, the pasture,

&c., and although one is bound to keep in touch with all these matters, the actual work of dealing with them is all done by J. M. junior.

Sometimes the missionary is bound to hear some of the 'cases' arising out of these matters, and how I have groaned over the interminable talks involved in such cases! As a rule, the only way is to pray for patience, and to listen to every one's version from beginning to end, but just occasionally fortune favours one with the means of a summary decision. On one occasion there was a big dispute between some of the Mission men and their neighbours over the border. The dispute concerned the number of a certain herd of cattle, and practically the only reasonable evidence was that of two rival herd-boys, who flatly contradicted one another. A happy thought struck me. I said to one herd-boy, 'How many men are there present here?' He counted, and, as I had guessed, he failed. The other boy having counted right at once, the decision could be given.

These cases between heathen and Christian are very much to be regretted, and for that reason one is sorry to see Mission land on which Christians are collected together. Border disputes with the heathen neighbours seem to be inevitable. Sometimes such disputes can be turned to good account, if only the Christians will speak and act as Christians. One day a case arose about J. M. senior's small son, who had been beaten by some heathen lads. I called a few Christian men and the fathers of the heathen lads. After a time the latter pleaded guilty for their sons, and said that they would 'tandazela' (beg off punishment) with a goat. This is a very common method of procedure amongst natives,

and the next step is for the person who has been wronged
to refuse until the offer is increased.   J. M. senior now
asked to speak, and, to my delight, when he had given
these men a good rebuke for shielding their sons, he
refused the goat and pardoned them.

I should only weary my readers if I attempted to
describe the innumerable ways in which these two men
put themselves at the disposal of the missionary for the
benefit of the community at large.

I am thankful to say we have many laymen all over
England, in town and country, who give up time and
brains in the cause of the Church and of charity.   I hope
that some such men may read these few words about
J. M. senior and J. M. junior, and will rejoice that what
they themselves are doing for the Church at home, men
of another country and of another colour are also doing
for the infant Church in Kaffraria.

. . . .

Some time after I had written the above, I had a letter
from a native Priest in which, speaking of J. M. junior,
he says, 'He is laid up again.   In Kafir we should say,
"He disappears and reappears like the moon".   It is
wonderful how that man is attached to the Mission.
The Doctor had advised him to go up country, but he
says he dreads being landed at a place where there would
be no Church services, and where, if he died, he would
not be buried by the Priests of his Church.'

CHAPTER X

ISAAC MAGUDU

FOR a long time I knew that a few of the Christian men on the Mission were holding meetings together at different kraals, but the object of the meetings seemed to be a secret. I felt sure, from the character of the particular men, that the meetings were for good and not for evil, so I held my peace. One day I received an invitation to be present at one of these meetings, which on that particular evening was to be held at the kraal of Alban Maka, one of our old Pondomisi boarders, who was then a catechist.

At 8 o'clock, the time appointed, I walked over to Alban's kraal, and in the largest of his huts I found a collection of some of our Christian men, most of whom lived on S. Cuthbert's Mission.

In the hut stood a long table, in the centre of which was a little paraffin hand-lamp—of the sort which has no glass—from which proceeded much smoke, and scarcely any light. Round the table on forms were grouped the members of this meeting (all natives), about fourteen in all, one or two teachers, one or two carpenters, one or two masons, and a few ordinary peasants without special trade.

At the head of the table was James Madala, the ever-zealous churchwarden and preacher, who has been our right hand for many years.

At the other end was the subject of this little story—

Isaac Magudu—a strongly-built, kindly-faced man in Deacon's Orders, and aged thirty-eight.

I particularly asked the men to carry on this meeting just as though I were not present, as I wanted to be simply a witness of the proceedings.

Magudu the Deacon then began with reading a short passage from the Acts of the Apostles, and saying a few words of explanation. Then he read some prayers and intercessions—especially for the conversion of the heathen —and I think we then sang a hymn.

Now began the regular business of the meeting, and my curiosity was very much aroused when I saw James Madala produce a big book, and heard him read out the names of a number—perhaps sixteen or eighteen—of men. Those who were present answered to their names, and came forward to place upon the table varying sums of money. When the name of an absentee was called, James pulled out a letter from a packet in front of him and read it aloud to the assembled company. In each case the letter contained either a money-order or else a promise of one.

This was becoming rather mystifying to me, and I began to hope for a speedy explanation. According to the regular rule of the Diocese, all these men were already contributing a fixed sum quarterly to the support of the Church's work, and they also helped by their donations to build the various church and school buildings, but this seemed something altogether apart.

At last the explanation came, and it was very sweet to my ears.

The prime mover in the matter had been Isaac Magudu, but he had been well backed by James Madala and one or two others. These men had attended a Native Conference two or three years previously, at which the whole question of the financial position of the Church had been discussed. It was urged then that we ought not to be satisfied with the measure of self-support which then existed. It was not sufficient that large Christian congregations should be independent of English money; the work should be regarded as a whole, and the Christian communities should not feel satisfied until their contributions flowed over to support the evangelistic work amongst the heathen.

At the time I remember thinking that this sounded like a counsel of perfection, and that the day of its accomplishment was rather far distant. However, the words spoken at that Conference were not fruitless. These few men, at any rate, put their heads together, and formed a sort of guild with tentative rules, the object of which should be (1) to stimulate the desire for the evangelization of the heathen, and (2) to provide means for the support of such work. Apparently they had agreed together to contribute a regular amount quarterly, and their rules did not allow that this money should be used until it reached the sum of £100. When it should reach that amount, the officers of the Guild would give it to the missionary to be used in the support of a catechist or preacher amongst the heathen. Their hope was that one of their own number would be so engaged, and that his work would then receive their support.

There were other interesting details in connexion with the rules and practices of this Guild, but I am not now concerned directly with the Guild, but with the prime mover of it. A man who, in spite of the pressing claims of a very large family and the limitations of a very small income, could originate and throw his heart into such a movement is one whom we like to know better. We have probably always heard that the Kafirs are noted for cupidity and avarice, and we hardly expect spontaneous self-denial and generosity to find birth in a Kafir kraal.

But if we do find this, surely it may help us to recognize and acknowledge the reality of conversion and the power of Christ in the hearts of men.

Magudu was born in 1867, the year in which a diamond was first discovered in South Africa. The poor farmer whose children were playing with that famous diamond, which was afterwards laid on the table of the House of Assembly, little knew that he had in his possession the magic wand which would change the whole fortunes of the Colony.

Let us hope that the happy omen may be fulfilled! Magudu's intellect certainly does not sparkle with the brilliancy of a diamond, but his heart is good, and his love for others is potent for great results.

His parents were heathen, and his father died as such, but his mother eventually followed her son into the fold of Christianity.

In Magudu's case I suppose we may again trace conversion back to the influence of a good master—an Englishman. He seems to have been about eighteen when he left his home and entered the service of this gentleman, who was then magistrate's clerk at Maclear. He remained with him for about six years, and his master seems to have taken a genuine interest in him, and to have given him some education. What a difference

REV. ISAAC MAGUDU.

To face page 101.

it must make in the life of a Kafir when his employer is a good Christian, and feels some sense of responsibility for his servant!

Back into the heart of heathen Kafir-land come Kafirs now from work amongst Europeans, bringing with them blatant atheism, as well as novel forms of vice[1].

Where employers do not treat them as though they expected them to have any degree of self-respect, what can one look for but moral ruin? In European towns they are no longer hedged in by the social restraints and customs of their own people, they no longer have an outlet for their animal spirits in the recognized ways of their own race, and often they have not the support even of the 'expectation' of their employers—they are not expected to be moral.

Magudu's career seems to have been a particularly varied one, and at different times he has been interpreter, constable, waiter at an hotel, groom to a Roman Catholic Bishop, and a sawyer! It is not many of us who can boast of such a variety of occupations!

Although he was influenced in the direction of Christianity by his first master, his step out of heathenism is another instance of the Kafir's belief in dreams. The dream seems to have vividly impressed him with the fact that man has no permanent home here on earth, and that he must seek one elsewhere; whereupon he put himself under the guidance of those who preached of that other home.

After his baptism he married a daughter of our old friend Kanyelwa Mpazi, who was then the preacher at Esiqunqwini, and he was subsequently invited by Bishop

[1] See Kidd's *Essential Kafir*.

Gibson to settle at S. Cuthbert's Mission, in order to receive more training for definite Church work.

It was there that I first made his acquaintance in 1891, and for the next twelve years he was more frequently my companion than any other of our native Christians.

At various times he went about with me as interpreter, but his usefulness was certainly not limited to that particular work. I often think that the Kafirs are the most extraordinarily patient people. The kind way in which they submit to experiments in their language without a murmur is truly wonderful.

Often and often I have no doubt that Magudu and I between us came hopelessly to grief in our joint efforts to bring home my words to the people, but certainly our united action was better than my unaided attempts of early days.

I remember on one occasion when I had barely been two months in the country, I was visiting one of the out-stations for the regular monthly services. To my dismay I found that there was no one in the neighbourhood who could interpret for me. I could just manage at that time to read Evensong and to celebrate the Holy Communion in Xosa, but all preaching and all intercourse with the people were out of the question.

It may be imagined that I was somewhat thrown off my balance when an infant was brought into the little church by Christian parents to be baptized. I felt that as the visits of a priest were necessarily infrequent it would not be right to refuse, but, just as I commenced the service, I was suddenly tortured by the thought that the question of sex might make a difference in the wording—and how was I to determine that matter? At last I thought I remembered the correct words, and, emphasizing the tone of interrogation, I asked—pointing to the infant—if it were 'umfazi' or 'indoda'?

Dead silence followed, and my torture became more intense. Eventually light dawned upon some brilliant person in the congregation, and I caught the English word ' boy', and proceeded.

It was only afterwards that I discovered I had asked if the infant were a married man or a married woman!

Many such grotesque incidents could be recorded, but that one shall suffice to explain that, without Magudu or some one like him, the situation in those early days was not an easy one. One felt so hopelessly isolated from the people, and so much of a mere machine when on a visit to an out-station one could administer the Sacraments, and do nothing else.

Then, too, Magudu was so much of a real companion, as well as a means of intercourse with the people, and I can look back upon many, many happy days spent with him, when the weariness of the journey or the difficulties in the work were wonderfully lightened by his constant cheerfulness and unselfish consideration for others.

Among the Kafirs, who are very fond of giving nick-names, Magudu was always known as 'Freepass', a name which was no doubt a reminiscence of his days as a constable, when he used to examine the ' passes '.

They used to know him as an official of the Government, with uniform and revolver, whose arrival in their kraals too often betokened the seizure of their goods for hut-tax or fine. How strange to see him now in cassock and surplice coming amongst them with a burning desire,

not to take, but to give—coming to listen to their difficulties, to counsel them in their sorrows, to pray with
them in their sickness!

Some of us, however, used to speak of him not as
'Freepass', but as 'the thirsty one', because of his
extreme avidity for lectures and 'notes'. Often when
my eyes have been heavy, and my body tired—and
when Magudu ought at least to have been equally tired—
he has come with an eager look to know if there would
be any instruction! I thought of my Wells days at the
Theological College, and I felt ashamed!

I am quite sure Magudu very often used to 'plough
with my heifer', and indeed I quite encouraged him to
preach my sermons, because I knew that he would
improve upon them, and transform them into 'Kafir'.

Often dear old Bishop Key used to say to me, 'When
you preach to Kafirs, think of a blacksmith beating a
red-hot piece of iron. Think how he turns it from side
to side, giving first a blow on one side, then on the other;
so you must turn the subject over and over, again and
again.' That is certainly an art which Kafirs themselves
possess.

In course of time Magudu passed from Reader to
Catechist, and from Catechist to Deacon, but although
the joys of the prefix 'Reverend' and of the round
collar were very great, yet he never thought too much
of his dignity, and was always ready to take his coat off
and to take his turn with the plough or with anything
else that needed a good strong pair of arms.

I must confess that in two particulars he does not
shine. First, his 'music' is very indifferent. Some of
my brethren would probably use a stronger expression

about it. I have noticed a look of the most abject
resignation on the face of one of my brother priests
when it has chanced that Magudu has struck upon a
favourite chant. As a rule the Kafirs are naturally
musical, and they have a wonderful way of taking their
parts correctly without an acquired knowledge.

Secondly—forgive me, dear friend!—his reading is
poor, and when he comes to a word or passage which is
unfamiliar to him, he plunges into the deep of the
unknown, and hopes for the best!

But what comparatively small matters these are—oh,
that all our faults were merely such matters of the
surface!

At present Magudu is at an out-station called Gqaqala.
(Beware, O reader, of attempting to pronounce that
name until, after long practice, your tongue can imitate
fluently the popping of a cork without pausing in the
pronunciation of the word!)

What a different thing it is for the priest to go to
Gqaqala now that our friend is established there! I
remember so vividly my first visits to Gqaqala, when
I confess I found it nearly impossible to be cheerful
except at the expense of banishing thought.

The fault was not so much in that tumble-down little
sod church where we used to hold services, nor in the
hut where we used to sleep, nor in the uncertainty about
food supplies, as in the seeming inability to get into
touch with the people, and, to all appearances, the
extremely surface nature of their Christianity.

When we arrive there now there is, to begin with,
a very hearty welcome from Magudu and his wife Emily.
Then there is a nice hut all made ready, and possibly

a cup of tea after the long ride.   Then there is a solid stone church with its well-ordered sanctuary, and, best of all, there is the evidence that the plough is no longer merely scratching the surface.

Let me end by telling the vision of my hope about Magudu's future.

There is a certain place where the population is almost entirely heathen.   In that place is a hut which is used both for services and for school purposes.   There is a preacher there whose intentions are good, but his training very imperfect.   In my vision I see that that hut is gone, and in its place is a dignified stone church suitable to its Kafir environment.

In that church I see many, many of those people who were once heathen, now offering up an intelligent worship to the Father who made them.

I see Magudu, with a stole no longer round one shoulder only, and he is standing at the Altar offering up that most acceptable and holy Sacrifice which our Lord commanded us to offer in memory of Himself.

CHAPTER XI

NOFAMILE NOHOLOZA

WE have been told, and yet we very often forget, that 'the Kingdom of Heaven is like unto treasure hid in a field'. We walk over the field and blame it because it is only a common field and we see no treasure, but sometimes we find that our eyes were at fault.

Just now I was writing of Gqaqala in days gone by, when I first knew it, and I said that its Christianity seemed so very much a surface matter.

No sooner had I finished writing than a vision of old Nofamile Noholoza came before me, and at once I felt rebuked.

I will not now alter what I said, but here I will write at least a qualification, if not a condemnation of my words.

It must be nearly two years since old Nofamile was called to rest, and my knowledge of him dates from a good deal longer back still.

Most unexpectedly and fortunately, it seems that a kind friend has kept some letters of mine to him in which I wrote about Nofamile. Passages of these letters appeared in the *Cowley Evangelist*, and I cannot now do better than quote them as they stand.

In my first letter I wrote as follows :—' My thoughts run often to Nofamile Noholoza just now. I suppose it is because he is ill, and I too happen to be *hors de combat*. When I saw him, he was sitting on a goat-

skin, wrapped in a coloured blanket, outside his hut.
He did not tell me that he wanted anything; it was
only some days after my visit that I heard quite accidentally that he was very poor and had nothing. . . .
He is an old man living at Gqaqala, one of the out-
stations of this parish. For years he has regularly made
his Communion at our monthly visits, but beyond this
I did not know much of him. I do not even remember
whether he is a convert of recent years, or whether
I found him here as a Christian.

'Hearing he was very ill, I walked over to his kraal
from our priest's hut, and found as I have described
above. I sat down by his side and asked to hear about
his sickness.

'"I am ill," he said, "but it is the will of God I should
be ill, and the will of God is good; it is the only good
thing. God is the only living one, and we all have life
from Him."

'I told him that with this faith he need not be afraid,
he could not be overcome, and he answered: "How can
Satan overcome, when he himself is already overcome
by our Lord when He rose from the dead?" (I felt that
there was nothing in his words of the self-assurance
which jars upon one, but simply a real confidence in our
Blessed Lord's Atonement.)

'I then read the Gospel for the day, and talked about
it to him. It was the warning against over-anxiety—
pointing to the birds of the air and the flowers. As
I spoke I was wondering how much the old man was
understanding. He had never learnt to read a line, and
knew nothing except what he had heard in instructions
and sermons, but he had evidently responded to the grace

of the Sacraments, and here was the secret of his understanding.

'Nofamile waited until I had finished, and then said: " I am a fool (a man of no understanding) and a corpse (meaning a dying man), but even I can understand these words, they are beautiful words—words of life . . . the treasures of the world do not help us . . . how can they help us ? I have nothing, I trust in God alone." '

Perhaps it was more the presence of the man than the actual words which impressed me so deeply.

In another letter I wrote :—' I must tell you one more word about Nofamile. Brother —— went up to the place where he lives for a meeting, and started with the preacher to seek a sick person. Their way led past Nofamile's kraal, and then the Brother, who had never seen him before, saw a little old shrunken man sitting outside on a stone.

'On their return a thick cold mist came on, but as they approached Nofamile's kraal, they heard him singing—sitting outside on the stone as before.

'They listened, and heard a few words of his song, which were to this effect : "A Child has come into the world. The Child has no sin, but comes among us sinners. He comes for our sake ; He comes to His friends, and His friends receive Him not . . ."

'I found out the other day that one of the preachers some forty miles away, was a son of Nofamile's, and asked him about his father. It was evident that the son had a great reverence for him, and he told me that it was a frequent habit of his to go out on to the veld at night to pray to God.'

Another letter adds :—' I visited Nofamile to-day, and

hope to celebrate at his kraal to-morrow morning. I found the old man sitting outside the same hut, on the same goat-skin as at my first visit two years ago. He is less able to get about, but more unconquerably joyful than ever. He has hardly any eyesight left, and yet his face looks quite radiant.'

Yet another letter says :—' Nofamile came tottering up, with the help of his stick, to make his Communion this morning. After the service he came to our hut, and began by saying that he " never thought he should meet me again in this world, but ——" he pointed up with a smile on his face to the world where he really seems to be living.

'After breakfast we had a meeting with the men about payment for the new church, for which each man had been assessed at 7s. 6d. To our great surprise Nofamile went up to the chief and put a sovereign in his hand as his contribution. Where he got it from is a mystery, as he is known to have nothing, and is consequently excused all hut-tax by the Government, as well as church assessments. Possibly he had been given it by one of the young men of the kraal who had worked for it " at the gold-field ".'

May I now quote the comment made upon these letters by the recipient :—' Here is a life as low in its circumstances as you could well find, and here is the mystery which changes all things, the Christ by the Word and Sacraments coming to the man as he goes through his vale of tears, and leaving him radiant within, while the external gloom and sorrow remain.

'Here is joy in the Lord in a life emptied of every other element of joy—joy associated with humblest penitence, with liberality abounding out of deep poverty, with a habit of frequent communion with God alone on the mountain and in the Sacrament, and with manners cheerful, gracious, and simple—joy in such companionship attests the mystery of the Incarnation—Christ coming into the individual soul that welcomes Him, and changing it into His own likeness.'

CHAPTER XII

MARITA

A MODERN writer has said that 'the regeneration of society is in the power of the woman', and I believe this is very largely true not only of London, but of Kafir society in the Transkei.

It was a great loss to the Church's work at Esiqunqwini when Kanyelwa was taken away to the Leper Asylum at Emjanyana, but fortunately there was another person in that place who exercised a great influence for good, and the name of that person is Marita. I so well remember the last time I saw and talked with her. I had been ill, and it was thought that it would be good to get into the fresher air of the mountains above the Mission.

It happened that our friend and neighbour Mr. Erskine had built three Kafir huts on the top of the hill behind Somerville, and he very kindly put these at my disposal.

In two of these huts I took up my abode, and a Kafir woman, who went to cook for me, occupied the third. My cook had a little girl for her companion, and I had Nino, the fox-terrier, for mine.

It was rather a lonely spot, and the only human beings we saw were the women who came up from below to get firewood in the forests beyond our huts. These women always walked, as is the custom, in single file, and very often as they neared the forest they sang the weird chant-song which seems to stimulate them for their plunge into the dark and solemn wood.

But one day I saw two women approaching who were dressed, not in the red-ochred blankets, but in European clothing. They both walked as though they were tired, and presently I recognized them as Marita and another Christian woman from Esiqunqwini. They had heard that I was ill and that I was staying somewhere in the mountains, but they were not quite sure of the exact locality, and they had taken five hours to reach my abode. And why had they come ? For precisely the same kindly reason that you would go to leave a card with kind inquiries at your friend's house in the neighbouring street.

Marita has a dark skin, and lives in a round hut, but she has the instincts and manners of a lady.

At once I called out to Rebecca the cook to boil the kettle and to make some tea, but Marita heard me and deprecated the trouble on her behalf just as naturally as you would have done. If only we take pains to look through the superficial differences between the races of men, we shall find that the real humanity underlying these differences is very much the same all the world over.

Marita began to tell me the last news of Kanyelwa from Emjanyana, of the progress of the Mothers' Union at Esiqunqwini, &c. Then she asked me how I had fared in the great gale which had swept the country a week or two previously. I pointed first to the miles of black burnt veld all round us, and then to the new thatch on one of the huts. The old roofing had been blown away, and during my absence of a few days, nineteen

Christian women from the Mission had come up, without my knowledge, and had re-thatched the hut. 'Those are the things', I said, 'which make us thankful to be here.'

As I spoke I thought of the many kind things which Marita too had done and was doing at Esiqunqwini, but I did not tell her of my thoughts.

After a short time Marita and her friend set off for their long walk home, and I little thought that it would be so long before we should meet again.

Now that I have introduced you to her, let me tell you something more about Marita and her early life.

Her mother was one of the lesser wives of a Fingo named M., and, until her childhood was well past, Marita was brought up among entirely heathen surroundings.

M. was not a chief, but he must have been a man of some position. His first wife was the 'great' wife, and her hut would, according to universal Kafir custom, be built immediately opposite the entrance to the cattle kraal. Marita's mother, being the second wife, would be called the 'right-hand' wife, and her hut would be on the right-hand side of the 'great' wife's. M. also had a third or 'left-hand' wife, whose hut would be on the other side.

In the case of a chief, polygamy is still more complicated by the fact that each of these wives has allotted to her an 'iqadi', or lesser wife (literally the 'rafters' which support the roof), whose children in some way belong to her.

It takes a long time before a stranger can come to know at all intimately the affairs of a heathen kraal. A little knowledge is often dangerous here as elsewhere, and it frequently happens that the public is presented with a picture either very much too white or else very much too black.

Undoubtedly there is a great deal that is attractive in the primitive character of the people, and in their social customs. They are an affectionate people, with a great deal of natural courtesy, and with large instincts of hospitality. Their habit of sharing food with all comers, even when the crops have failed and grain is at famine prices, is worthy of all respect.

Again, it is delightful to find that there is no such thing in fact as an orphan—although there is the name. No Kafir child bereft of parents will at any rate want for a home, or some one to call 'father'.

Characteristics such as these are the foundation upon which missionary work must be built. But, on the other hand, there is a great deal which is very horrible about life in a heathen home. I remember some years ago, an old clergyman in England drawing me aside and saying, 'I hear that the primitive Kafirs are a very moral people, is it true?' Undoubtedly there is a certain amount of truth in it. The social and family life is protected by a very rigid law of ownership. But of morality in a Christian sense, there is practically none.

Perhaps the greatest curse of heathen life arises from a belief in, and the practice of, witchcraft. The daily chant of heathen life is a sort of negation of Psalm xci. Wherever the unseen touches upon human life, it is the touch of hatred, or anger, or punishment. The witch-doctor is one who has dared to learn the secrets of occult art in order to ward off malignant influences. The more these influences are multiplied, the more scope there is for the witch-doctor. Witchcraft is called in at every stage of heathen life.

No sooner was Marita born than witchcraft was doubtless called upon to set its mark upon her. At least she would be adorned with the necklace charm made from a few hairs pulled out of the tail of a certain cow.

Until she could walk, she would be strapped on to her mother's back by means of the upper blanket, and would in this way accompany her mother on long walks to the forest for firewood, or to the ploughing lands when hoeing or reaping were to be done.

Dolls seem to belong to 'nursery life' all over the world, and although it is certain that Marita never received one penny to spend upon such a luxury, she doubtless manufactured the usual doll out of a mealie cob, and loved it as much as if it had been wax-made with moving eyes.

At a very early age she would become nurse to a baby-brother or sister, and a little later would be sent to the lands to drive off birds from the ripening corn.

At the time when childhood begins to pass into man-hood or womanhood, no words can describe the degrading character of the customs still in force amongst the heathen. A recent writer—not a missionary—concludes some references to these rites with these words, 'It may be safely said that nothing is left undone which could be expected to destroy any lingering remains of self-respect in the girl's mind.'

This was the nature of Marita's home-training, but at this time a very remarkable change took place in that home.

SMALL BOARDER CHILDREN.

To face page 116.

It seems that M.'s three wives became attracted by the preaching and prayers of some Christian people, and in course of time they all three became converts. It would be interesting to know how M. took this at first. In all probability he was very angry, and endeavoured to uproot Christianity from his kraal. It is, however, remarkable to notice how quickly the sincerity of a convert wins respect amongst the heathen. If the convert is anything of a hypocrite, the heathen relations are the first to see and to resent it; but where there is reality and steadfastness, opposition generally dies away.

In this case it was not long before M. followed the example of his wives and became a convert.

Here was now produced one of those very difficult situations with which the missionary is constantly brought into contact. M. was a convert anxious to be baptized, but he had three wives. What was he to do? The answer to this question has not always been the same, and latterly there has grown to be a very strong feeling that the wives in such a case ought not to be put away until there is the possibility of doing so without any risk of harm and wrong to them. In this case the husband would remain for the time unbaptized. At the time of which I am writing, the difficulties of separation were not seen with equal clearness, and M. was told to put away two of the wives in order that he might marry the remaining one with Christian rites. But which wife? M. loved Marita's mother, and wanted to keep her; but obviously it was his duty to marry the ' great' wife, who was ' par excellence' *the* wife. Both Marita's mother and the third wife seem to have seen this, and to have acted with the greatest decision — leaving the kraal until M.

actually married the great wife. Then they returned, and M. built homes for them in the neighbourhood.

What a strange chapter this must have been in Marita's life, and how one would like to know the impressions made upon that small mind! Apparently she was at least influenced in the direction of Christianity, as it was not long before she herself became a convert. As is so often the case, the final step was brought about by a dream in which she seemed to see messengers bearing a message to her from God.

We must remember that Kafirs have a firm belief in the instrumentality of dreams for good or evil. The dream became to Marita just what the star became to the Magi of old. She immediately told her mother, and went to the preacher to declare her conversion. Eventually she was baptized by Archdeacon Waters, and confirmed by Bishop Callaway.

She now married, and became Marita S., but was soon left a widow with two children. It was as a widow that she came face to face with the great temptation of her life. I do not know many of the particulars, but it is clear that she was an attractive woman, and that her attractions cast their spell over a young man belonging to the chief's family.

This man had a Christian wife living, from whom he was separated, and Marita knew it. The temptation was too strong, and she agreed to become his wife. Apparently there had been no civil recognition of the man's previous marriage, and she went with him to the magistrate's office to go through the form of legal marriage.

Strange to say, neither the real wife nor the husband lived long, but while the latter was still living—his wife having died—Marita became a penitent, and her marriage was duly blessed. One son was born, and then came the sorrow of another bereavement by which Marita again became a widow.

There is something particularly desolate about widowhood, or indeed any bereavement in Kafir life. This is well expressed in the 'Song of the Afflicted', which I quote from Mr. Kidd's book on the *Essential Kafir*.

The women cry :—

> We are left outside,
> We are left for sorrow,
> We are left to despair,
> Which increases our misery.
> Oh, that there were a refuge in heaven!
> That there were a pot there and a fire!
> That there were found a place for me!
> Oh, that I had wings to fly thither!

The widow adds :—

> Oh, foolish woman that I am,
> When evening comes I open my window[1],
> I listen in silence, I watch,
> I fancy that my husband returns!

Then all the women chant :—

> Alas! are they really gone?
> Have they left us here?
> But where are they gone,
> That they can return no more
> To see us again?
> Are they really gone?
> Is hell[2] insatiable
> Will it never be full?

Christianity alone can drive away this darkness, and give to life a 'new song'.

[1] A hole above the door.
[2] Hell is the cavern in the earth where the dead go.

In the recent report issued by the South African Native Affairs Commission, it is said—speaking of the results of missionary work—' There is growing up an ever-increasing number of self-respecting native women, who are learning to understand the freedom which has come to them, and are careful not to abuse its privileges.'

All I would claim for Marita is at least a place in the forefront of this band.

In every parish in England there are some women whose lives are an inspiration to many. One can think perhaps of the widow of a country squire who lives on in the old home, actively employing herself in good works, visiting the sick, and helping the poor.

Allowing for very great differences in the circumstances, Marita occupies in her humble home at Esiqunqwini a somewhat similar position. Of course she works on her own lands like the other women, does her own washing, and cooks her own food. There is no back-door and front-door entrance to her house, she is probably no richer in cattle or sheep than the majority of others in the place. But if any one is in trouble or sickness, if there is any quarrel or disturbance among the Christian people, it is to her that people naturally turn, and I do not think they turn in vain.

Marita's widowhood has been a long one. I have known her for fourteen years, and she lost her second husband before I knew her.

As one sees her in her daily life, in her place in the church, in her intercourse with others, one feels that the victory of the Cross has been hers. I do not say that she is a saint, or a heroine, but I have always felt that she is one of those people whose daily life is a witness for Christ.

CHAPTER XIII

JAMES

At this time James is a man of about forty-eight years, a good honest Christian man, who owns a kraal on the Mission and exercises a real influence for good.

It has often seemed to me that the story of James's life ought to be very interesting, and, now that I have leisure to write it, I only regret that I am 7,000 miles away from first-hand sources of information.

All his childhood must have been passed in stirring and adventurous days, when the war-cry was never long unheard. He must have seen changes of the most momentous kind, affecting the whole life and well-being of the Kafir tribes.

I began to ponder over the facts with which I was familiar concerning his life and conversion to Christianity. Presently it seemed to me that the 7,000 miles had vanished, I was no longer at Mayens de Sion, facing the snow-capped mountains, and looking down upon the Rhone Valley. I was sitting outside James's kraal at S. Cuthbert's Mission. I was looking down from the ridge on which it is built, to the little stream which runs to meet the Ncolosi.

Over on the other side were the Mission buildings, and the stone walls of the fine new church.

Sitting by my side was James himself, and at last, it seemed to me, I had persuaded him to tell me of his early life. Bit by bit, out it all came:—

'I am only an unlearned person. We natives are not like white people—we do not keep books. I do not even know how many years have passed since my birth. Those were days of darkness, Mfundisi [1], our eyes were not then open. We are a very slow people, and even to-day we do not believe. The Government is wise, he [2] is our father, but we think he is an enemy.

'The Government told us to be vaccinated, and we shut our ears ; then the small-pox came and ate us up.

'The Government told us to dip our sheep ; still we did not believe, and then the "scab" spread, and we began to listen.

'Again, the Government told us that rinderpest was coming, and that we must inoculate our cattle—once more we were fools, and our cattle are dead. It is not easy for a people like us to believe.

'The missionaries are not the Government, but they too are our fathers. They tell us many things which we do not understand.

'Some of us think that all white people are alike, they do not see that missionaries are not like other white people. They say, "Where are those oxen which our chief once sent by the hand of a white man to the Government?" [3]

'When I was a boy we had only heard of the white

[1] Name for missionary.
[2] The Government is always 'he' and not 'it'.
[3] It appears that Mditshwa, the late chief of the Pondomisi, was at one time anxious to come under English protection, and actually sought to make representations to this effect to the authorities. He collected some cattle, and handed them over to a white man who undertook to deliver them and the message. It is to be feared that neither cattle nor message were ever delivered.

man, and we thought that every white man had come
to "eat us up".

'I was born in the year when Umhlakaza declared his
message—the white man stayed, and the black people
died like locusts [1].

'Well, it is difficult to say why we are called Pondomisi.
Some people say that we were the "izimpondo", the
" horns " of the southward movement of the Bantu races.
More probably, we were called by other tribes the
Pondos of the old chief, Umse, and so came to be known
as the Amampondomisi.

'In the days when I was born our tribe was living
between the Umtata and the Bashee rivers. In those
days Mditshwa was a great chief. Many were the

---

[1] One of Kreli's counsellors, named Umhlakaza, announced that
he had received a message from the other world. It had come to him
through his daughter, Nongqause, who professed to have seen the
spirits of the old heroes of the tribe. They had announced to her
that they and all the dead warriors of the race would appear once
more in the flesh to rescue their nation. Their coming would be
preceded by a whirlwind, which would sweep off all the English.
The sun would rise blood-red, and at noon suddenly descend to
the east. Out of the earth would rise vast herds of fat English
cattle, food, guns, &c. Living men and women would resume the
bloom of youth, and the race would be gifted with immortality.
The spirits demanded, as a condition of their appearance, that
all cattle must be slain, every grain of maize and corn must be
thrown away, and the land must remain untilled.
If Kreli did not invent the prophecy, he encouraged it in order to
force on another war. For months the slaughter of cattle went on.
Grain was destroyed until none was left, and the people began to
suffer from famine. At last the supposed resurrection day arrived.
The cattle kraals had been enlarged to receive the expected herds,
the corn pits were cleared out. . . . A dreadful period of famine
followed, in which some 30,000 perished.

stories I heard of his brave doings. Sometimes some
of us herd-boys, when we had shut up the cattle safely
in the kraal, used to hide ourselves and listen to the men
talking of the wars.

'Our enemies were many; on one side the Pondos, on
the other the Tembus. Both these tribes had larger
"impis" (armies) than our own. The warriors used to
say that before engaging the enemy they would watch
Mditshwa's face, and when he smiled they knew it
would go well. When I was still quite a small boy our
tribe was at last driven out, and we were forced to
retreat to these parts between the Inxu and the Tsitsa
rivers.

'For many years after this I remember nothing but the
sound of war. It was soon after this time that the gourd
was split right into two[1]. The two halves both hold
milk now, but at first it seemed that the two sections of
the tribe would swallow one another up.

'Our chief, Mditshwa, never disputed that Mhlonhlo
was the paramount chief, but he said, "My people are
mine and not his."

'It was at this time that we first heard of a missionary
coming amongst our people. One day there arrived at
the "Great Place" (chief's kraal), at the Tsolo hill, two
white men who had come to see the chief. Mditshwa
was away on a visit to some people in the Drakensberg
Mountains. Our people can do nothing without the
chief; they can only put their hand to their mouth until
the chief has spoken.

'No one knew why these white men had come. Some

thought that they had come to sell us blankets, and hoes, and beads, and they were very glad, because many people had not got these things. Messengers were sent to call back Mditshwa, and when he arrived there was much talking. We then heard that the white men had come to live amongst us, and that Mditshwa had consented to their coming.

'The white men then went away, and after a time we said that they had only spoken words, until one day the news came that they were on the mountain above the Inxu, looking for a way to bring down their waggon.

'Mditshwa gave them a place to build on, by the banks of the Inxu river, but at first we were very suspicious of these men. Some people whispered that they were men who did not like the laws of their own country ; others, when they saw them receiving people accused of magic, said that they were witch-doctors. It was only after a long time that we knew that we had with us a great chief—a white man with a black heart [1]. Even then we did not understand what he said.

'One day we heard that the Government was going to protect us and to rule over us. The people did not understand what this meant, but we heard that Mditshwa was glad, and that he said we should no longer be eaten up by our enemies. He knew that the great white Queen was very strong, and that it was good to be her child. That was a time of great change. We see to-day that it was good, but yet we say it was not all good. We were only children, and we did not understand all the words of the Government. Mditshwa used to say that the Government took away his people from him. He had gone to

[1] An expressive way of denoting sympathy.

the Government with the people on his back [1], and the
Government ought to say " his " words to him, and he
would say the words of the Government to his people.
Even to us it did not seem good that men could run
round the chief to go to the magistrate.

' We think of these complaints to-day when we remember Hope's war [2].

' That was a bad thing which Mhlonhlo's men did to
kill the hand of the Government. We are sorry that
Mditshwa joined in that war.

. . . .

' You want me to speak about myself, but I do not
know what to say. I was like every one else. Some
time after the war, I went to ask Nqubantwana [3] to let
me build on his land. At this time I was married.
I was the eldest son of my father, and he had many sons.
We all went to live under Nqubantwana.

' Often I used to go away to work for the white men,
and one of these times I was driving the waggon of our
magistrate. This man was a very good man. Some of
the things he did made me think. Before his food I used

---

[1] In the way that a mother carries her child.

[2] In 1881, Mhlonhlo, the chief of the other section of the tribe,
agreed to meet Mr. Hope, the Magistrate of Qumbu, at Sulenkama.
Mr. Hope went to the appointed place with only three English
companions and two or three native policemen, and he and his
companions were cruelly murdered. The Pondomisi then rose in
rebellion, but were finally crushed. Mditshwa was taken prisoner
to Capetown, and Mhlonhlo, after hiding successfully for twenty-
four years, was captured last year, and after a long trial was
acquitted of the actual murder.

[3] A petty Pondomisi headman, who was rewarded for loyalty in
the war by the gift of a farm.

to see him stand up and say some words. I knew that
he was speaking to u-Tixo, the Great Father of whom the
missionaries tell us.

'I thought much about this. It seemed to me that it
was good to speak to the Great Father, and if our food
was given by Him, it was good to thank Him. It was
quite clear to me that we Kafirs knew nothing.

'We put the seed into the ground, but who gave that
seed life, we did not know.

'Sometimes I was afraid to think much of these things.
I was afraid that perhaps I should be caught and com-
pelled to become a Christian [1].

'But the thought of God never left me, although it was
eight years before I gave myself to Him. Often during
those eight years I used to pray in my hut to God, and
sometimes I used to listen to what the preachers and
others said. At last it seemed to me that I was like
a man who comes to a river and is afraid to cross. He
wants very much to get to the other side, but the water
makes him afraid. There were many things which made
me afraid of becoming a Christian.

'I knew that a man must be a brave man to fight
against many of the customs of our people. What should
I say if my father became sick? Could I refuse to call
in the witch-doctor and to make a sacrifice [2]?

'While I was thus hesitating, many things were happening round about me. For a long time there had been
two or three Christians near by, who had always walked
to a place far off, for their services, but now a large hut

---

[1] The allusion is to the belief among the heathen that converts
are made sometimes by magic.

[2] This would be the recognized duty of the eldest son.

was built in Nqubantwana's location, in which a preacher and teacher began work. The same thing was happening in all parts of the country. Although u-Key (the late Bishop) was no longer amongst the Pondomisi, he had left others to carry on his work, and the seed which he had sown was now beginning to bear fruit.

'Some of our people began to see that this work of the missionaries was not to be feared—perhaps even it was good.

'"But", they said, "this thing is for our children, it is not for us. An ox must be trained for the yoke when it is young."

'The witch-doctors still hinted that the work of the missionaries would ruin the tribe. They pointed to the long drought which had caused so great a famine, and they laid the blame upon "this new teaching".

'At this time, too, one of the new converts lost her only child. Her husband had never agreed to her conversion.

'When she went to wash her blanket [1], he had beaten her, and she had said, "You may make me smear my body, but you cannot make me smear my heart."

'Now that she had lost her child, the witch-doctor said that the case was quite clear. She had killed her child by the new magic.

'But the woman was very brave, and did not give up her religion.

'This, too, made me think very much. I asked myself, What makes this woman so brave?

'Then at last I felt that I must not wait any longer. In a battle, if a man strikes, he may conquer, or if he runs

---

[1] The red-ochred blanket has become the badge of heathenism, and the convert immediately washes off the red ochre.

away, he may be saved, but if he hesitates he is a dead thing.

'I went to my box and took out some clothes which I used when I went to work amongst the white men. I put these on, and I then went to see the preacher.

'He said to me, "Are you well?" I answered, "I am well in my body, but sick in my heart." He said, "What makes you sick in your heart?" I answered, "God makes me sick in my heart." He said, "God makes men sick that He may heal them."

'I do not remember other words which were said that day, except that the preacher said I must come on a certain day to see the missionary.

'I went home that day, and called my wife. I said to her, "I want you to go to the river to wash my blanket." She said, "Your blanket is new." I said, "I will use it when it is white."'

CHAPTER XIV

THE SCHOOL AT NQOKWE

ALTHOUGH not mentioned by name, Mdunyelwa has already appeared in these stories. It was he who came into the trader's store, and made himself responsible for the purchases of the less prosperous among his men. If you are prepared for a rough ride of two and a half hours from the Mission, I should very much like to take you to see Mdunyelwa's home at Nqokwe.

For much of the way our path leads us through the plough-lands upon which the prosperity of the people so much depends. On the ridges above the lands are the Kafir kraals, looking always so entirely indigenous to the soil. They seem to be just as natural a product of the country as the big brown ant-heaps which are met with everywhere. Even the people in their red-ochred blankets are a note in the harmony.

After a few miles the country becomes wilder and more rugged. You are obliged to give up hope of another canter, as the path now winds about the rocks of a steep mountain-side. The aloes, with their dark green leaves and their bright red flowers, add just the touch of colour which is wanted. Below, in the valley, is the winding Inxu river, and its banks are cultivated to the very edge. At last Mdunyelwa's home is reached, and your horse is gratefully led away to be ' off-saddled '.

The kraal is built on a rocky ledge of the mountain,

looking down on the junction of two valleys where the waters of the Nqokwe flow into the Inxu.

Many and many a time I have sat out in front of the kraal, talking with Mdunyelwa and some of his men. Preachers have gone there Sunday by Sunday for many years, and often I have tried to persuade the old headman to take a more decided step forwards, and at least to have a school in his location.

At the back of his mind I believe the real objection was this—' When the Government wants us to do anything, " he " does not ask us whether we would like to do it, he says, " You must do this ". If this thing that the missionary says is good, why does not the Government call us together and say " You must build schools, you must support preachers, and so on " ? '

Of course Mdunyelwa would never tell me the real reason, but he always managed to find another.

Although, for a long time, these meetings did not seem to effect their immediate purpose, yet they were probably not without some good results, and certainly they never lacked interest. Sometimes, before the talking began, old Mdunyelwa would put his hand into the thatch of the hut (inside), and pull out a roll of papers. With an air of great solemnity he would bring these to me, and ask me to read them for him. First, I would come to a Government document, telling of some meeting to be held, or of some law recently passed, and these would require much explanation. Then would appear a bundle of advertisements of some patent medicines—' Mother Seigel's Syrup ' or ' Pink pills for pale people '. All the usual stories of grateful patients who had been given up by all the doctors and had at last found magic relief—all the detailed list of symptoms of the various diseases, to which poor human flesh, black as well as white, is liable, would be set forth in these advertisements in a 'tongue understanded of the people'.

What a strange puzzle all this must be for the poor unlearned Kafir mind! It is very difficult for us to forget the twentieth-century Englishman, and to penetrate into the mind of our old friend Mdunyelwa when it comes to the matter of the written alphabet. These are days when pens have multiplied to an alarming extent, and we are daily deluged with rivers of ink. In the face of the present alarming literary output, it is more than ever necessary to 'try the spirits' whether they are true or false.

And yet it is not so long ago that even in England one could meet with educated people who believed every word of their newspaper.

The Kafir has been transplanted into a strange land of learning which is wholly new to him, and hitherto a thick mist of ignorance has for the most part veiled it from his sight. But the mist has been lifting here and there, and he sees tiny fragments of the new territory. Is it to be wondered at, that he tries to judge of the unseen by the seen? In the place of his chief giving his decisions according to well-known custom, he sees magistrate and lawyer hunting through a book. When the book speaks, the case is finished.

When he is called to the 'great place' of the Government to hear a new law, the magistrate stands up with a paper in his hand. When that paper has spoken, there is no more to be said.

When the preacher, who is the 'hand' of the missionary, comes to him on a Sunday, he holds a book in his hand.   It is that book which speaks, and the preacher only has to ask him to open his ears and listen.

It seems that men must always be silent when the 'incwadi' (the word is the same for book or paper) speaks.   Even when the trader sends round his written ' demand ', there is nothing to be done except to obey.

As yet the question of the authority lying behind the words of the book must be very vague and hazy.   Why should not ' Dr. Williams ' and ' Mother Seigel ' be just as infallible as the writers of the Roman-Dutch law, or even as the Bible itself?

This question was surely a good text on which to build my arguments for a school.   By the time that I had finished explaining to Mdunyelwa the contents of his post, his men would have arrived and the meeting would begin.

The Kafirs are good listeners, but sometimes, when the talking is long, a little secret conversation is carried on, and this is known by the delightful expression ' skinning a mouse '.   I suppose the idea is that the big matter for which the meeting is called is like skinning an ox, which requires the hands of many men.   In comparison with this all private matters are like the skinning of vermin.

At one of these meetings at Mdunyelwa's home, I remember seeing two men ' skinning a mouse ' over the tag of my boot-lace.   They evidently admired this as a great work of ingenuity, and I heard one of them say to the other, ' Why ! with a thing like this, a man could put on his boots in the dark.'

After many meetings and many promises, the school

was at last agreed upon, and a large round hut was built
for a beginning. The Mission paid for the building and
furnishing of this hut, but, as is usual, Mdunyelwa and
his men were required to collect and repay the amount
at an 'opening meeting '. Oh, those opening meetings!
How they tire the missionary! In this case it was of
course a small matter, but where the building happens to
be a large one and the sum required runs into three
figures, the meeting seems to be interminable.

The natives' method of giving at these meetings is
peculiarly their own, and I do not think it is to be
wholly commended.

I have no objection to gifts of cattle, sheep, goats, pigs,
fowls, &c., but the speeches which are considered to be the
necessary prelude to each gift might be dispensed with.

When it happens that a man multiplies these speeches
indefinitely by bringing a pocket full of small cash—each
coin representing a speech—the missionary requires more
than the average amount of patience. As I think of
these meetings, innumerable scenes of humour rise up in
my mind, and dispute the claim of 'weariness' to the
first place assigned to it by memory.

I can see now an enthusiastic old lady of vast dimen-
sions and strangely juvenile attire, sitting in the front
row of the assembly. She had come armed with a dona-
tion of twenty shillings, and most thankful I was that
apparently she had been unable to divide them into
'tickeys' (3d.). By her side was a man who ploughed
her lands, and acted, in the absence of her husband, as
a sort of farm manager. On this occasion he was
specially retained as speech-maker, and, at a given signal,
up he would get to herald the offering of each of these

twenty shillings. I doubt very much if his agricultural talents equalled those of his tongue!

Again, a vision rises up before me of a certain meeting called to provide £50, paid for the building of a small church.

It was whispered to me that a certain prosperous chief had promised to come, and to bring some of his men with him. This was regarded as a considerable asset, and the interest was perceptibly great when the chief and his party hove in sight.

Room was at once made in front, and the chief, attired in an old military over-coat, took his place. Some audacious person now stood up and said, 'We are all very glad to see chief —— at this meeting, and I give 1s. to thank him for coming, and to open his mouth.'

The gentleman in the military coat now stood up and made a long speech, at the end of which he dived into one of his huge pockets, and produced two pennies which he laid with great ostentation upon the table in front of me! My feelings were only partially mollified when, later on, he gave the promise of a sheep. Nothing short of an ox could have quite pacified me!

The day was at length fixed for the opening of the school-hut at Nqokwe, and I determined to make as much of it as possible. Several of our leading Christian men at the Mission kindly agreed to go over there to encourage the people.

The meeting was to have taken place on a certain Saturday morning, but, in spite of three messages to that effect, a mistake was made, and we arrived at Nqokwe to find ourselves expected on the following day.

There was nothing for it but to wait, and I fear the

men who accompanied me had rather a bad time. They got no food that day, and, having no blankets, they had to sit round a fire all night to keep warm. On the following day I celebrated the Holy Communion in the new hut, and later in the morning the heathen people began to arrive. First came the women, carrying cooking-pots and baskets of grain on their heads. Then came carcases of sheep and goats, intended first for the cooking-pots, and afterwards to reward the donors for their liberality.

It is an understood rule on these occasions that no food is to be touched until the giving is concluded. It is thought that the pangs of hunger will stimulate generous instincts.

At last Mdunyelwa himself arrived, and the meeting formally began.

The spot was a most picturesque one. We sat in a sort of hollow sheltered by rocks and thorn trees. But before the 'giving' commenced the sky became very angry-looking, and ominous puffs of wind would catch up dry bits of grass and whirl them round. Reluctantly I decided that we must go inside the hut, and by dint of great pressure we all crowded in. The wind now became more and more fierce, and we glanced fearfully at the roof, as a stronger blast than usual would move it on the walls. On this occasion I do not think I was the only one to feel that speeches had better be curtailed.

Old Mdunyelwa, who is in many ways a real gentleman, opened well by quietly putting £1 upon the table without saying a word, and he was followed by his son with another pound. This was a good start, as we only wanted £9 in all, but it could not be expected that such a high level would be maintained, and we had soon dropped to gifts of fowls, dishes of grain, tickeys and coppers. Eventually, after a rough calculation, I was able to announce that the amount had been realized, and then I went on to tell them an important piece of news. Let me here tell this piece of news in different words:—

About twenty years previously a son of a Pondomisi of good birth named Sodinga had been brought to my predecessor, Canon Gibson, to be trained, together with the son of the chief Mditshwa. The boy was very bright and attractive, and became popular, not only with his teachers but also with many amongst the Pondomisi. At his baptism he received the name Chelston, and great hopes seem to have been entertained about his future.

Long before my arrival at the Mission, Chelston Sodinga had disappeared. Like a certain young man of whom we read, and very like the man we know best in our own selves, he came to dislike the restraints of the 'father's home'. Not seldom heathen life calls to those who once knew it with a most constraining voice. When the vision of its alluring charms· is in the eye, other interests seem dull indeed. Through the school windows come the strange notes of some distant dance-song. Immediately the school with its desks, and slates, and maps, vanishes away. A new scene is conjured up. A sudden taste of the food which gladdens the heart springs to the mouth. Bright eyes flash, mocking words are heard.

Strange it would be if victory were always on one side.

Where Chelston had gone I did not hear, but as the time passed by and he did not reappear, I quite gave up all hope of seeing him again. An old lady in England who took an interest in him used to write to me that she felt sure he would return, but she did not live to hear that her prophecy came true.

One day, about three years ago, a man whom I did not know came to see me, and in a few minutes I found myself listening once more to the tale so often told. The 'far-off country' had again proved inhospitable—the love for the real home had been only dormant and not dead. Chelston Sodinga had 'come to himself'.

Great was the satisfaction in the home of Mdunyelwa when I brought forward Chelston at the meeting, and told the people that he was to be the first teacher of their children.

QUARRYING AND CARRYING STONE FOR THE NEW CHURCH.

To face page 139.

CHAPTER XV

THE NEW CHURCH

I WAS sitting out one morning on a mountain-side in Switzerland when the whole landscape was blotted out by a thick mist. I tried to put myself into the position of a stranger who might find himself in that place for the first time. In vain he would speculate about the nature of the country before him. Were there mountains, or forests, or fields of cultivation, or habitations of men? Question as he would, that impenetrable mist would give no answer, and a strange feeling of helplessness would creep over him. Suddenly, as I sat there, a minute opening is made in the mist as if by some invisible hand. Right through that opening peeps out a lofty snow-covered peak framed in a fragment of blue sky. The mist still blots out all the rest from sight, but I am no longer in the presence of the unknown and unknowable. That peak seems to invite friendship and to promise a further revelation.

Did I, at this point, wander into dreamland? or was it only a rapid flight of imagination?

I found myself sitting in a stall on the north side of the temporary chancel in the new church at S. Cuthbert's[1]. I was leaning my head against the last of the stone pillars on that side, and looking up to the clerestory windows opposite. My mind travelled back

---

[1] At the time of writing, the church is yet unfinished. Scaffolding still surrounds the walls, and the roofing is only begun.

to the early history of the building. All the ups and downs, the hopes and the disappointments, came back before me. I thought of the first beginning, more than eight years ago, when a few native men were set to open a quarry. Then came the various efforts to train our native lads to cut stone and to build. Throughout all the years flitted ghosts of an empty cash-box.

A curious feeling of satisfaction came over me as I realized that now the work of years was complete. The roof was on, and it mattered not how hard the rain might beat or the wind might blow.

I looked round the building with joy, and then I saw that the whole church was filled with a large congregation. No room was left in nave or aisles, and even the floor of the church and the steps of the immersion-font were occupied by people.

Many were the familiar faces, but it seemed to me that not a few of these had changed very much.

Some of those whom I used to know as heathen were there, but something about their faces and manner seemed to tell me that they had been buried with Christ in the waters of Baptism, and had risen with Him to newness of life.

Some whom I had left as children had become young men and young women, and eagerly I looked to see what traces the last two years had left upon their faces.

Suddenly the whole congregation rose up, and, when I too had stood up, I saw standing on the chancel steps a native priest whom I knew well. He made the sign of the cross, and said, 'Ngegama lo-Yise, nelo-Nyana, nelo-Moya Oyingcwele' (In the Name of the Father, and of the Son, and of the Holy Ghost).

We all sat down again, and he began his sermon. At first my attention wandered, but all at once I found myself listening to every word.

'Once', he said, 'we were all living in a thick mist. All we saw was the ground under our feet. We were born, we became conscious, we grew up, we hunted, we made war, we ate, we drank, we laughed, we cried, we suffered, we died. No one asked " Why are we born ? " " Who made us ? " " Where do we go to ? " Yes, we heard the stories of Unkulunkulu, the great, great Father, who is said to have created the world. We said, perhaps it is true and perhaps it is not true. We thought little about it. We were glad that the mist was so thick and that we could not see. We said, evil and misfortune are behind the mist, we do not want to see any further. Sometimes, when sickness or sorrow came, we said, it is the work of the enemy behind the mist. We called the witch-doctor, and we told him that he must propitiate the enemy.

' Then some of us saw the mist lift. It was just as if the door of your hut were suddenly opened in the early morning, and you looked out of darkness into light. In the opening before us we saw one lofty mountain-peak. When we saw that, we were no longer afraid. That peak which we saw is Jesus Christ. The mist still hides many things from our eyes. Even the most learned men cannot see very far into it. But Jesus Christ has much to tell those who see Him and seek to know Him. He is the Word of God. Being God Himself, He makes known God to us in a way which we can understand. When the white man first comes to us, we cannot understand what he says. His word is strange to us, it

tells us no more than his silence. But he finds an
interpreter who knows both his language and our own,
and then we can understand. Jesus Christ is the interpreter. He is the perfect interpreter because He is
perfect God and perfect man. He knows the mind and
the language of God because He is God. He knows the
mind and language of men because He is man. He does
not speak to one race of men only. He did not take the
person of one man or the nature of one race. He took
the nature of all men, and He belongs to all races.
When we see Him we are no longer afraid of this mist
of darkness which hides so much from our eyes. We
see that there is indeed an Unkulunkulu (great, great
Father), not of one race but of all. We see that He is
not an enemy, but a Father. Yes, we know that the mist
hides bad things as well as good. We know that
there are enemies as well as friends. But the good is
stronger than the bad, the friends are stronger than the
foes. When sorrow and sickness come to us here, we do
not send for the witch-doctor. We do not say it is the
work of an enemy. We look to Jesus Christ, and we see
that His Countenance is always full of love. If He heals
us, it is good for us to be healed. If He does not heal
us, He has some better gift for us than healing.

'But Jesus Christ does not only tell us about God, He
has also much to tell us about ourselves. He lifts the
curtain of mist which hides us from ourselves. In Him
we learn what a nation ought to be and may be, and
what a man ought to be and may be.

'To-day is a day of great change. The old customs
are passing away. The civilization of the white man
has come amongst us. It is breaking down many of the

walls which our fathers had built.   Some of those walls
were good, and some were bad.   Who shall tell us which
were good and which were bad?   It is Jesus Christ who
will tell us.   In Him we belong not to one tribe only,
but to the great family of new-born men.   He tells us
what things are to be kept, and what things are to be
put away.   Nothing that is good is to be lost.   We read
that some people brought little children to Christ, and
that He laid His hands upon them, and blessed them.
We, too, have to bring whatever is good in our tribe to
Him, to be blessed by Him.   When a man goes to the
" store " to borrow money, he knows that he must pay
interest upon that money.   We have borrowed the great
wealth of the Catholic Church.   We must not only use
that wealth, but we must also pay the interest.   God
expects us to bring something into His Church, something even more than we received.   As we stand here in
this new church, let us go back in thought to the days
when the mist first began to lift.

'I will not speak now of the days when Bishop Key
first used to preach to the Pondomisi on the banks of the
Inxu river.   I think rather of the time after the war,
when he came here to this place (S. Cuthbert's) and
made an " umzi " (home).

'In those days a hut was built for the service of God.
That hut, outside, was just like all the other huts in
which people live.   But it was there that some of you
first saw the mist of darkness begin to lift.   It was there
that the peak stood out in the blue sky.   That hut has
passed away, but its work is still here.   The builder of
that hut has also passed away, but we remember him
to-day with thankful hearts.   The name of Bransby

Lewis Key will never be forgotten amongst us. We see the small stone font which he cut with his own hands, and the altar which he made out of wood grown in the forest at S. Augustine's. Those are amongst our treasures in this new church, but they too will pass away. There are some things which will not pass away. Some of us owe to him our first knowledge of God, and upon our heads we still seem to feel the laying on of his Apostolic hands. After him came "u-Gibson", now bishop at Capetown, and none of us can forget the power of his example. It was new to us to see a man become quite poor that he might make others rich. We began to learn what those words meant about giving up parents, and wife, and home, and possessions. We saw amongst us a priest who never spared himself. It was in the time of "u-Gibson" that another church was built to take the place of the old hut. That church has had a life of twenty years, and we do not leave it now because we do not love it. We feel to-day rather like the daughter who is leaving her parents' home on the day of her marriage. Although she loves her husband and wishes to go with him to the home he has prepared, she finds it hard to leave the old home. We find it hard to leave the old church where we have learnt, and received so much. But when a child becomes a man, he requires the clothes of a man. This congregation has grown until now it can no longer find room in the old church. Eight years ago it was clearly seen that we must prepare to build a new House for the service of God. Slowly but steadily has the work gone on from that day to this. Often our hopes have almost failed, when we saw how great was the work and how many were the difficulties. One thing we are

THE NEW CHURCH—WEST END.

To face page 145.

chiefly thankful for to-day is that our own sons have been
trained to do this work. It is they who have laboured in
the quarry, and have brought out the stones. It is they
who have patiently squared and shaped all these stones,
and have built them into these walls. To us this work
is almost like a miracle. We have never seen such
a thing. We thank God to-day for those men who have
come to teach our sons. We hope that they will have
learned much more from them than to build in stone.
We have seen men who work for the love of God, and
not for money. We hope that our sons will learn, too,
that nothing is so great as to live and to work for the
love of God.

'My friends, I will end my sermon by quoting some
words which were told me to-day by Father Godfrey.
One day he was telling some kind English friends about
this church at S. Cuthbert's while it was being built.
Three little children belonging to these friends heard
what he was saying. When they said their prayers that
night, one of them prayed "that nothing may prevent
Father Godfrey's return to Africa . . . and that the
church which he began to build may be a home to many
people, and that all those who enter it may grow in
goodness and grace[1]." To this prayer we may indeed
all say Amen.

'Now unto God the Father Almighty, His only-
begotten Son Jesus Christ, and to God the Holy Ghost,
be all honour, glory, power, and dominion, now, hence-
forth, and for evermore.'

---

[1] These children, although English, say their prayers in French,
and I give a free translation.

APPENDIX[1]

WORK AMONG THE NATIVE RACES OF SOUTH AFRICA

THE old danger of disregard of the claims of missionary work seems, to some extent, at least, to be passing away. The leaven of a rich enthusiasm is certainly working, and this new-born fervour not only infuses itself into the Church at home, it also makes itself felt in the missionary field. Speakers who have recently spoken glowing words at meetings of the Junior Clergy Missionary Associations little knew how far their words would carry. Certainly here in South Africa they brought to some a consciousness of humiliation and a real longing to rise up to a higher sense of privilege.

Many of us who have been missionaries for years know how fatally easy it is to drop down into a settled groove, and to let slip early visions of evangelistic zeal. We know how easy it is to become accustomed to heathenism until we almost forget that we came to overcome it by the power of the Cross.

Those words from the old country have come like a gust of wind upon the dying embers, and one wishes that more could be done to join hands across the sea with those who have come to our rescue.

Such enthusiasm will not, one feels, falter in the presence of difficulties and dangers; and perhaps it is just here that we missionaries may play our part in the new crusade. We do know the dangers and difficulties

[1] Reprinted from the *Cowley Evangelist* of Oct. 1902.

of the mission field. We do see the weak points in the Church's warfare, and we may be able to forearm the leaders of the new enterprise if we venture to whisper our warnings out loud. This is my chief reason for writing, and I hope my words may do nothing to quench enthusiasm, and may do a little to strengthen it.

In this part of the mission field it is a time of great changes, and there are signs in all directions that the tide has turned towards Christianity. With the turn come many new problems, which did not present themselves so forcibly to our predecessors. It is quite possible that many priests who are working in English parishes may be aroused by the new enthusiasm to offer themselves for work in these parts. Think of the case of one of such men. He has been doing perhaps up-hill work in some English country parish. He has learnt there how slow the most real success is. He has become rather afraid of rapid outward results. He has seen that solid growth seems to depend more upon the steady faithful work amongst individuals than upon the attractive sermons and other agencies which work in a more wholesale way. A priest such as this offers himself for missionary work. It is very difficult for him to form very clear conceptions of the work for which he has offered himself. He has heard lectures and read books about the country, but imagines that for some considerable time after his arrival he will be simply in the position of a learner, and will have ample opportunities of acquiring the knowledge of the people, their language and customs, upon which his future usefulness will depend.

He comes out, and hardly has time to look about

before he is plunged into responsibilities, and he is dimly conscious, as he struggles along, that he is doing something day by day to lay down lines for the wheels of the future.

To a certain extent the position of the early missionary pioneer was easier and clearer. He came to live amongst a heathen people, and for a long time his work was bound to be rather indirect. He had to live amongst them, to get to know them, and to win them to know him. He became, perhaps, counsellor and father of the people long before he began to dip them into the waters of Holy Baptism. Church discipline, and all the intricate questions connected with the abandonment of the heathen social system, were as yet in the future.

Thirty or forty years have passed, and now our priest who comes out from England finds everything completely changed.

The canons, it is true, may demand certain qualifications before a priest can be put in charge of native work, and those in authority may recognize the tremendous importance of such a condition, but necessity overrules the law, and the priest is put down in charge of a parish as large, perhaps, as an average-sized English county.

What does he find there? Probably a certain amount of European work. Two villages, perhaps, twenty miles distant from one another, and containing ten or twelve families of English people. Then, too, there is a certain area in his parish reserved for European farmers, and amongst the natives he finds scattered English traders. From these he turns to a large native Christian population, perhaps amounting to thousands, scattered about all over the district. These people belong to different locations, and in each location there is a chief or headman, who has certain control, to be exercised under the authority of the resident magistrate.

In each location where there are many converts, our missionary will find some sort of church and school buildings, and some degree of organization. At most of these centres he will find a native catechist, or preacher, and a teacher.

Now let us stop for a minute and face the responsibilities involved in these two classes alone—the Christian European and the Christian native. Obviously they have the first claim upon him. The children must first be fed.

Probably he will find it necessary to give all his Sundays to the English work, as well as the necessary visits on other days to people scattered about. Subtract the time thus given to the English folk, and will the remainder be sufficient for effectively meeting the wants of the native Christian population? I think not, but I will not now try to answer that question.

There is now a third class, which forms the bulk of the population resident in the parish. This is the mass of heathen natives which occupied the chief place in the eye of his imagination at home. These were the people to whom he was to be sent, and upon them his thoughts and prayers had been fixed. Here they are more numerous even than he had ever imagined. He has to ride through them day by day. He has to pass their kraals and to see their red blankets adding a touch of colour to the view in every direction. And yet in a sense they seem further away from him than before. He does not forget them. He does not willingly neglect them. In a sort of way he does work amongst them, but it is second-hand work. Between them and him is constantly forcing itself a large undigested mass of work, which demands more attention than he can give it.

Now here it is that I touch upon, to my mind, the first great danger in our work. It does seem of very great importance that the missionary should get to know the heathen. I do not dwell upon the importance of their getting to know him. That can hardly be over-estimated. It is sometimes a real delight to see the confidence heathen people have in a man because he is a missionary. They have learnt to expect courtesy and faithfulness to promise from a missionary, as well as a regard to their interests, and I can remember the time when an act of theft from a missionary was spoken of with horror by heathen people.

But naturally the missionary must not remain a mere official if he is to exercise a real influence over them. They must get to know him personally, and for this purpose he must get to know them. But surely there are other reasons why a first-hand knowledge is of the greatest importance. The new lines cannot safely be laid down without an intimate knowledge of the old.

The state of change is always a dangerous one, but never more so than in this great change, where one by one the members of a heathen nation become converts to Christianity. Must there not always be a certain danger that our converts may come from the number of those who belittle law and custom, and therefore carry the same spirit into the Catholic Church?

How necessary, then, it is for us to have a knowledge (and with knowledge comes respect) of the laws and customs amongst the people in their heathen state.

A stranger, looking merely from outside at the homes of the people—the beer-drinks, the fights, the heathen rites, and the general absence of any outward garb of law and order—might easily conclude that all was irregular, and that individual misdoing and indulgence would be the natural order of things. That heathen man whom he meets staggering home from a beer-drink, with his red blanket thrown over his shoulders, how can he enforce order in his large home?

I suppose it takes a lot to persuade us that there can be order without a full-dressed policeman and the regular procedure of the magistrate's court, but such a conclusion is quite a mistake.

For generations and generations a social and family system has been growing into being amongst the heathen. It is a system not dictated by the revelation of God, but largely based upon the known needs and rights of men. Any one with any knowledge of the Kafirs recognizes at once the remarkable excellence in some respects of much that is visible in this social custom.

It is perhaps impossible to define the difference between our laws and customs and those of the heathen tribes. Outwardly our laws and theirs recognize and punish much the same offences, but there is a great difference between the ideas which lie behind the laws. There may not be much actual recognition of religion in the outward administration of English law, and yet behind all is the belief that man belongs to God. Amongst the heathen this is absent, and we find only

the recognition of man's ownership. The rights of pro-
prietorship are very strongly stamped upon the heathen
mind from the very earliest years. The little heathen
boy grows up with a full knowledge of the penalty of
theft. He dare not steal a handful of tobacco, and, if
he does, he counts the cost. One may say, in fact, that
'Thou shalt not steal' is the one commandment of
the Kafirs. Every other offence seems to be in some
way classed under the heading of theft. The severest
consequences of all attend a theft of his neighbour's
human property—his wife or his daughter. The consequence is there is a wall which is built round passion,
and it is a strong wall.

Our converts, then, come from a social system which
has in it much which must be the foundation on which
we build. They are our children, and come to be taught
by us. But we do not want them to separate from past
obligations and old customs, where there is nothing con-
trary to the mind of Christ. We do not want to say to
the father of a heathen family, 'Your children are ours,
you have nothing more to say to them.' Nothing would
be more fatal. We should be killing the very moral instincts upon which we are to depend in building up the
convert in the Christian faith. We should be bringing
upon ourselves the reasonable reproach of all that is best
in heathen life. We should be losing our best chance of
influencing those who still hold back. We are rather to
join hands as far as is possible with the father of the
heathen family; we are to emphasize our respect for the
moral obligations, and try only to lift them up into
a higher atmosphere, and stamp them with a divine
authority. When I have sat sometimes listening to

a heathen headman hearing a case of moral wrong-doing amongst his people, I have felt that I can gladly support every word he says. But what a difference it would make if only he were *consciously* upholding God's law and not only man's!

Now it must not be thought that I am dreaming of accusing the Church as a whole of ignorance of what is good in heathen life, nor must I be thought to be joining in the cry of those who on this very account condemn missionary work. My one purpose is to urge that to enable the Church to do what she wants to do, and what she sets before her to do, her hands must be infinitely strengthened, and her missionaries multiplied.

The Church takes a very clear line in her canons and regulations. She has been guided by wise and faithful men, who spent their lives in acquiring the knowledge which is now at our disposal.

With the canons of this diocese are published some general directions to the missionary, and amongst them we read as follows: 'Missionaries should be careful not to interfere needlessly with harmless customs, or to act towards them as though they partook of the nature of sin.' Again, we read: 'It is very important that the system of rudimentary instruction for the heathen should not be given up; otherwise there will soon be found on each station a small and unprogressive Christian body of natives, separated and living apart from their heathen brethren; and the heathen portion of the population will come to be gradually overlooked and neglected.'

I believe this attitude has been completely misrepresented by many who have taken up popular objections to missionary work, but they may, I fear, too often point to failure to carry out to the full the ideals set before us.

Here is where the new enthusiasm must step in, and by men and prayer and alms supply what is lacking amongst us.